THE TRUTH ABOUT
DOWN SYNDROME

LESSONS LEARNED FROM RAISING A SON
WITH TRISOMY-21

ELIZABETH GOODHUE

ISBN: 978-1-7352814-2-1 (paperback)

Cover Design by 100Covers.com
Interior Design by FormattedBooks.com

To my father

Trisomy-21 or Down Syndrome?

Dr. Down is like Christopher Columbus. He was the first person to detect Down syndrome as a disorder. However, he didn't recognize it as a *genetic* disorder related to the twenty-first chromosome. As a result, this disorder is called Down syndrome, after Doctor Down.

Down syndrome doesn't deserve the negative connotation of Dr. Down's name. Down connotes negativity. I know it's a matter of semantics. Doctor Down didn't give himself his name, but he didn't get his discovery right either. It was Jerome Lejeune who identified Down syndrome as a chromosomal disorder in 1959, the year after I was born. Dr. Lejeune counted 47 chromosomes in children with Down syndrome, rather than the expected 46.

Imagine if the label Down syndrome hadn't stuck? Instead, we could use the etymology: "from trisome + ending from chromosome + y." The label, Trisomy-21, makes things so clear—three chromosomes. Unfortunately, changing the Down syndrome label is like changing your name. Everyone is so used to it. It would take constant reminding to get people to use the more appropriate term Trisomy-21, so that is why I use this term in this book.

Contents

Ask that Your Way be Long

When I chose to have children, I had it all planned. They would nurse, eat healthy food, be as free-range as possible, live carefree lives, go to public school, which I would supplement with nature, art, hiking, and reading volumes of Laura Ingalls Wilder and *The Lion, the Witch and the Wardrobe*. My children would learn to notice the world with insightful eyes. I would engage in their lives while letting them gain as much independence as necessary to survive in this world.

I had already moved to rural New Hampshire from Boston so that they could live in an environment similar to the one I experienced. As the breadwinner of my family, my staunch belief that babies should stay home with their mothers had already been shattered, but at least I had chosen the right profession. As a teacher, I could spend vacations with them when they started school. I was excited about sending them to public school where they would meet people from diverse backgrounds, unlike me, who had spent my elementary school years in private school. From there, their opportunities would multiply as they approached high school and graduated to college and beyond. My children would have it all.

I found out that life isn't so predictable when William was born with Trisomy-21.

William's entry into the world took all night—as if the universe was deciding whether to let him in or let him go. When he entered this world, he didn't cry. He flopped over his folded legs as he would for most of the transitions he made later in his life before feeling ready for what came next. A pause hung in the air a little longer than felt right as if to say, "Wait a second. I need to think about this." If I had known William as I do now, I would have expected this. I would have been the first one to breathe.

Suddenly, everything became medical, and after some whisking, scooping, and juttering about, William started to breathe. The obstetrician's shoulders sagged with the relief of having finished with his obstetrics. Nurses fluttered like fireflies stuck in a jar before they took William from me to inspect him and give him a shot of vitamin K. Even though the 8:30 morning sunlight should have broken through the dusting of snow we had that morning, the room was dim.

I am no different than any other mother who recognizes that raising children is the most challenging thing a woman can face. Children bring out an extraordinary emotion that touches the core of a mother's spirit and body. William was no different from his sisters, Kate and Claire, in that way. Each child presented me with the challenges children do for working mothers—daycare, the perils of middle school, chickenpox, facing an animal's death. William's trials took more oomph on my part—hospitals, advocating for the best education he could get, and transitioning out of school into the world. I have grown used to the stares and outlandish statements following us around as if William is a curiosity. I may not have skirted the obstacles I had to face for William with grace, but I learned how to navigate the journey as each one presented itself.

Welcome to
Holland

Emily Kingsley, once a writer for *Sesame Street*, has a son with Trisomy-21, which is the term I use for Down syndrome. In her 1987 essay, "Welcome to Holland," she compares his birth and her shifting expectations to landing in Holland when she thought she was going to Italy. In Italy, you would see Rome, the Leaning Tower of Pisa, the Sistine Chapel, and paintings by Michelangelo. Holland is flat, and all you can see are miles and miles of tulips and windmills.

When I was pregnant with William, I expected to land in Italy too. When he was born, and I realized he had Trisomy-21, I knew I was in for a long and arduous journey. On a bike, the headwind would be fierce, I didn't speak the language, and other than that, I knew nothing about Holland. I resisted the journey even though the plane had landed.

But I couldn't leave. William was William, not Trisomy-21. As I fell in love with him, I started to see things from a new perspective. Even though arriving in Italy was what had I expected—what I planned on—I had it all wrong. It took me some time to realize it, but landing in Holland was going to be okay. Certainly, there were some bumps along the way. William had heart surgery and an aortic repair before he was eight weeks old. The bureaucracies I would have to face spoke a different language. With William's birth, I had entered a new culture beyond the one I had lived in before. I learned a new language and saw life through a different lens. Still, after William was born, I started to notice a plethora of red, yellow, and pink tulips growing around us, and the windmills spinning through the day and night. I was, and am, meant to be right where I am with my beautiful child, who has given me far more than Italy ever could.

When you have a baby, any baby, especially your first one, all expectations fly out the window. Today, I embrace Holland. I see farther there than I see in Italy. In Holland, I watch windmills whir endlessly over fields of tulips of all different and extraordinary colors.

Unwrapped Packages

Trisomy-21 enters our lives like a gift packaged in brown paper. The paper is stiff, unyielding, and challenging to fold. Everyone unwraps the package differently. Perhaps with wonder. Maybe not knowing whether to laugh or cry, console or worry, send a sad note, or sing praises. More people than you would think aren't ready to unwrap the stigmas. Some people don't know where to put them once they open them. It is human nature to keep people in categories. Thus, extraordinary people are fit into the world in a particular way so that others can feel comfortable.

No one mentioned that William might have Trisomy-21 on February 22, 1989, the day he was born. Doctors and nurses skirted around us, focusing on his jaundice, and my inability to nurse him. Meanwhile, other mothers popped out pink baby girls and boys with healthy hearts who seemed to grow during their short overnight stays. People from my birthing class bounced in and out of the hospital. One mother concerned her daughter's ears might stick out too much, taped them down with Scotch tape.

William and I stayed in the hospital for days. I, still ignorant of the semantics, was sure he was a Mongoloid, an archaic term I am ashamed to write on this page. It took a whole day for me to gather the courage to admit the truth to William's pediatrician. When I did, she raised her eyes—perhaps because I was the one who said it first—as if I had opened the window and let in the fresh air.

Declaring my suspicion made it real.

Having a newborn son different from any child I expected to have, tore me apart. Guilt for not being elated, for feeling resentful and cheated seeped through my skin. Doubt wouldn't let me fathom how to make it through the next day, let alone the future. Devastation wrapped my heart. In the shower, I cried until my skin turned red. William was a mystery. He was also my son, which trumped everything, the doctors, my mother, Italy, guilt, fear, and doubt.

God and Angels

When people used God and William in the same sentence, it used to fill me with resentment. I brushed it away, but it resonated and fed my doubts about whether or not there is a God. A friend told me it was okay to be mad at God, which comforted me. It allowed me to be angry at something besides myself. Maybe God does choose specific people to raise children with disabilities.

A few days after William's birth, my Aunt Phoebe, whose daughter Susie has Trisomy-21, wrote, "God has sent an angel to you in William." Why would any god pick *me* for this job? From my perspective, the only thing God had done was send me a child I was incapable of raising. I was a first-time 31-year-old mother with a life-time of nurturing an extraordinary child ahead of me. Perhaps if I had known then what I know now, Aunt Phoebe's words would have resonated with me.

I wonder about God. I almost refuse to believe in him. Contradictorily, when things get rough, I blame Him, ask Him why he made me his new version of Job. Perhaps my formative years sitting on cushioned pews inside St. Matthew's Episcopal Church in Bedford, New York, molded these feelings. Even then, it felt uncomfortable praying to something as intangible as a God sitting in heaven with his flowing white beard.

Peering into the Future

When William was still recovering from jaundice in the hospital, I drove to town to take a break. I saw a man with Trisomy-21 riding his bike and weaving through the traffic. He was going places. Why didn't this man infuse me with hope? Instead, what lay ahead daunted me. How was I going to get William from where he was to where the man on his bike was?

I kept to myself because I was mourning for the baby I didn't have. During these times, I couldn't bring myself to call the women from my childbirth classes whose babies were going to go to daycare, pre-school, elementary school, and eventually college. Beyond that, their opportunities were endless. I wasn't sure that it would be that way for William.

When William entered the world, I felt as if we did not belong. One day after our prolonged stay in the hospital, I gave a ride to a colleague. She peered at William in his car seat. I felt compelled, as I always did, to explain he had Trisomy-21. She stopped me and said, "I know. He's beautiful."

She got it. She knew William shed light on what he held for us. We do belong here. I may feel alone in this world most of the time, but every once in a while, someone reassures me with their understanding and compassion.

Home

William arrived at our first house on Starrett Row in Bennington, New Hampshire, after spending his first week of life in the hospital with jaundice. Tom, my ex-husband, and I did not have the money to buy anything but this fixer-upper, with light pea-green vinyl siding, a one woodstove house. You could stand in front of a window on one side of it, and blow out a candle on the other side in one breath.

We hadn't finished turning the house from a shack into a home. Tom had built our bed and moved it to the second floor, which now had electricity and a crib for William. While I was pregnant, people used to ask me if I had decorated the baby's room yet. "Well," I would reply, "we put up the sheetrock this weekend, but we need to install the rest of the electrical sockets."

I was new to marriage, to homeownership, to making it from one paycheck to the next, to New Hampshire, and to parenting. I didn't know about the trials I would face over the next two decades, or that twenty years later, Tom and I would be divorced.

After William's birth, the depression I had lived with all of my life found an ample opportunity to surface and compound with the hormones and emotions wreaking havoc on me already. Depression creeps into me when life sneaks up on me unawares. It's exhausting. If I am not in the throes of it, I am in the throes of holding it back.

I grew up in a family of five. Three of us were and are bipolar. This led to my brother's death in his 50s. The three of us were sandwiched between a brother, who was seven years older than me and a sister who was seven years younger. Maybe it was birth order, perhaps it was me, but my parents didn't have the time or wherewithal to deal with another needy child, so I was the one who had to be strong. Falling apart was a sign of weakness. If any of us were sick, we kept quiet and went to school. I don't think I ever cried in front of my mother. I played sports with a vengeance and spent as much time as possible outside. As a child and an adult, I have sought refuge in nature and the woods to face my world. I worked hard to keep my lack of trust, my depression, and my vulnerability in check.

Cocoon Days

I was not new to feeling alone. I had spent a lifetime as a sole warrior, fighting my own battles and trying to understand how to live in a world that didn't make sense to me. However, with William, it was a different kind of alone and misunderstanding. After William and I settled into our house on Starrett Row, I spent most of my time alone—the kind of alone that comes with snowy New Hampshire cloudy days. Winter cold. Winter alone.

With William, I welcomed the quiet. I embraced the time I had to focus on him for days on end in all of the newness surrounding me. I pretended we didn't need to face the outside world. The heat from the woodstove curled through the dining room and found me in the rocking chair, holding William and falling in love. The heat was sparse, but enough to wrap us in the warmth of what was happening inside, where I could disregard the threats and realities of the outside world knocking on my front door. We weren't ready to metamorphose and fly headlong into the unknown. Now was the time to stay inside and rock, avoiding the cold raw days ahead.

The road passing by the house looked as grey and bleak as the sky. The neighbors weren't home, and the aloneness settled in like a quiet leaky storm spitting out specks of snow, silencing the birds in the eaves, and filling the house with loud, hollow reticence. In our house, I settled into my cocoon, where the grey February light streamed through the single window in William's room, leaving a small patch of warmth on the floor. The rocking chair sat in the corner. I could not afford to reupholster it, so I covered the worn, ripped, brown corduroy with a bedspread from my college days. It felt as if I was piecing my life together with the past because it was all I had.

William and I swaddled in the comfort of our nest. The snow still hugged the new March ground. Together we nursed, tucked under cover, protecting and loving more than I knew I was capable. Under the eaves, next to our nursing chair, a mother bird also made her nest. It was with her I came to know William. I wondered about the mother bird's experience. Perhaps, she was a Bluebird, or a House Finch, or a Song Sparrow. We had the same job to do. Both of us were protecting our young from the outside until they were ready to fly from the nest. I nestled into my cocoon trying to nurse William, while Mother Bird kept a pulse on the outside world, foraging for food.

I listened to her chirping chicks when she flew away to find food for them. William mostly slept and rarely cried. When Mother Bird braved the cold for her chicks, they kept each other warm in the nest. She would fly back and rustle in to satiate their cries for her and the food she brought. They stayed there with William and me, growing and becoming a part of our small world.

None of us was ready to leave the nest. While Mother Bird coddled her chicks, I rocked myself trying to get William to nurse, my old college blanket scratching my back with warm comfort. Compared to the chicks, William was silent, his skin soft, almost blue. I tucked his loose limbs into his blanket as I tried to feed him, not knowing I was barely keeping him alive. William slept more than he ate, and his breathing was labored. He was becoming more transparent each day.

Even though I didn't have to gather worms as Mother Bird did, I knew I would have to venture out of the nest too. I would have to step out of the house and lay a path for William, find a place for him to get healthy, and the right people to support him when I went back to work. A series of unknowns awaited both of us. But I knew the stories of baby birds falling out of the nest and never learning to fly.

I didn't have a chance to stop hearing Mother Bird's chicks chirping or when their chirping may have turned into song. I don't know when they started to fly from the nest or if any of them didn't make it. Maybe I stole away before she and her chicks did when I took William to Children's Hospital one day and didn't come back until the black flies were biting with a vengeance, the sun was high in the June sky, and her bird children swooped and dipped over the surface of lakes to satiate themselves without her.

Mustering Courage

In those first few weeks after William's birth, he slept, and I gathered my courage to call the first person who would start William and me on our journey into the real world. The world of "normal," if it would let him in. This contact would be my first step out of the nest, which I didn't want to leave just yet. Calling Jay, a daycare provider for William, took days of courage-mustering.

Before William was born, Jay had agreed to provide daycare for him when I returned to teaching high school in September. Jay took care of six kids at her house ten minutes away from mine. It took all the mettle I had to call her number. I dreaded she might not take him because he had Trisomy-21. I expected her to tell me that I needed to find a place that dealt with the Williams of the world.

"Hey, Jay, it's me, Elizabeth." I felt as if I had to explain who I had been before when William had been an expectation.

"Hello, Elizabeth. So, you must've had your baby by now."

"Yes, Jay, I did. That is why I am calling."

"That's great. Is it a boy or a girl?"

"It's a boy," I blurted out the rest, "but he has Down syndrome, can you still take him?" It came out in a garbled run-on so she would skim through my words without the interruption of a period or a semi-colon. I wanted them to gallop out of my mouth so she wouldn't have a chance to say no.

"Of course, I will. Why wouldn't I?"

I didn't hear the rest of what she said. William was going to daycare. He was going to do what any other kid would do when his mother went back to work.

First Steps

Amendments to the law were passed to ensure equal access to education for people with disabilities. In 1997 and again in 2004, the government passed additional bills to ensure equal access to education. With the advent of the Individuals with Disabilities Act (IDEA), school systems began providing Early Intervention. Early intervention supports children from 0 to 3 years of age with developmental delays or disabilities. It focuses on basic and new skills that develop during the first three years of life. The agency's name in our region then began its evolution to RISE. (sites.ed.gov)

Unlike other mothers, I also had to get William into the "system." Since William was a newborn, that system was Early Intervention. Early Intervention made William's Trisomy-21 a reality I couldn't hide from forever. During one of our many visits to monitor William's nursing and nourishment, his pediatrician advised that William needed extra support besides me and the "normal world." William was still a newborn, and I had another five months left of maternity leave. I hadn't realized that being with typical peers at Jay's house was the best education William could get. Already, William was struggling to nurse, and he continued to be listless, and he was not passing his "well-baby" visits. As a new mother, it was difficult to ignore the litany of the probabilities that could ruin William's life—leukemia, eczema, heart defects, mental retardation, Alzheimer's, early dementia—that *Babies with Down Syndrome* held in its table of contents.

I knew the Early Intervention program called RISE would take William. They had to. But calling RISE meant entering the domain of the disabled, a realm to which I didn't want to belong. I had become part of a community of people with whom I would never have crossed paths if it hadn't been for William. It was just as likely I would find myself at Loudon, New Hampshire's motorcycle rally drinking beer with a crowd of Harley Davidson riders.

I called RISE, to admit and commit to William's need for help. The woman who answered emphasized that this small window of time, ages zero to three, was *the* window. You miss *the* window, and who knows what could happen? He might not learn to read or walk or talk. RISE sent occupational, speech, and physical therapists to the house to tell me what to do. They set up balls, and swings, and mirrors, and toys that squeaked and squawked.

I did everything they told me to do. The pressure was overwhelming, not from RISE but me. My competitive spirit rose to the occasion. I started my quest to turn William into someone who could be all that he could be. Perhaps that is why he loves the military so much today.

When Trisomy-21 Switched from First to Second Place

William's Early Intervention was soon interrupted by a six-week stay in Children's Hospital Boston. He was one-month-old. William's inability to nurse indicated he didn't have the strength to thrive. At this time, I didn't know how healthy babies kept themselves alive without a struggle.

William was not a healthy baby, although, in my cocoon days, I did not know how unhealthy he was. He was my first child, and I believed people when they told me I couldn't nurse him well. As usual, I construed I was the problem, and, as usual, I persevered. I tried to nurse him to the point of delirium. Sometimes I woke in the middle of the night, and it took me a few minutes of hard brain work to figure out where I was, what I was doing, who I was, or that perhaps my dreams were my reality and not my life. My life turned into a hazy transcendent dance to another dimension.

William's Trisomy-21 switched from first to second place when I started slogging him back and forth to his local doctor. When he grew sick enough with what seemed to be a horrible cold, I called his pediatrician, Dr. Jean. Earlier, she advised me to supplement my breast milk with a bottle of concentrated formula, two tablespoons of oil, and no water. "How much do you think he drinks a day?" she asked me over the phone.

"About an ounce," I replied, knowing that was not enough.

"Bring him in right away."

Dr. Jean recommended we go to a hospital one and a half hours north of us to see a pediatric cardiologist. There we would find the renowned hospital where the big guns gave brave, gallant, always correct diagnoses, where the doctors would fix William, and we could move on with his life. It didn't take long to see that it was not going to be that simple.

Heading North

When we arrived at the hospital the next day, the cardiologist shook our hands briskly. He was a large man, one of many who would treat my tiny baby. The hospital was cold, stony, and dark. My shoes echoed ominously in the halls. When we got to the examination room, Tom and I consented to have a medical student observe. Then we wound our way through more dark hallways to a place where they would take a sonogram of William's heart.

I put William on a hard, plastic table covered with paper that crinkled and scrunched against his baby-soft skin and my sensitive ears. William squirmed and cried underneath fluorescent lights and the cold touch of this imposing doctor looming over him who sighed, "He won't stay still. We will have to take an X-ray." I plucked William from the scratchy, paper surface, wrapped him in his blanket, and held him close. I stayed with him for the x-ray despite the warning about radiation.

After the x-ray, we followed Dr. Giant and Mr. Medical Student through the next hallway to a puke-green room with a window that tried to compete with the fluorescent lights. This time, I listened to my instinct, and I climbed onto the crinkly-papered plastic examination table with William learning my first lesson along this dark journey to fix his heart.

The chit-chatting between the doctor and the medical student blurred through my brain until a nurse delivered the x-rays of William's heart. At this point, I had no idea of the magnitude this black and white image would hold. All I thought was that the doctors would find the problem and fix it. William was going to get better—in and out. Simple as that.

Meanwhile, Dr. Giant and Mr. Medical Student held the x-ray to the window to get a sharper view. "You see that?" Dr. Giant said to his mentee. "Right there, what do you see?" The medical student muttered something indecipherable. My inner voice screamed, *"what do you see? Show me!"* yet I remained silent in the shadows. I didn't want to know what they were saying. I needed to hold onto my innocence for one second longer.

I heard them say things like complete atrioventricular canal defect, open-heart surgery, typical in children with Down syndrome, set up a time for the operation. I looked at the doctor as I held William closer to my chest. I wanted to run away, but my hackles rose. "We are right here. Could you tell us what you see?"

"William needs open-heart surgery. When do you want to schedule it? You can call after you think about it, but it should happen in the next two weeks."

We wove our way out of the dark, cold, hospital castle, and made our way to the parking lot. It wasn't until we got onto Route 89 that I turned to Tom. "No one is ever going to treat us that way again," I said through gritted teeth.

The City of
Broken Hearts

A week later, when I packed William into his car seat, I expected another cardiology appointment like the one up north. This time it would not be a visit where I would hear a doctor diagnose him with his back to me. This time I already knew William had a complete atrioventricular defect and had a vague idea about what that meant. I also knew fifty percent of babies born with Trisomy-21 have heart defects. This time, I was going to tell his new cardiologist how he was going to be William's doctor. But I didn't need to. I had found William's healer at Children's Hospital in Boston.

After the appointment, I started packing William into his car seat to head back to New Hampshire. I asked his new cardiologist where I should go to make the next appointment. "Oh no," Dr. Flanagan replied, raising a thick eyebrow, "He is not going home. He is checking in." When I left home that morning, I didn't know we were going to stay there for six weeks. I found myself with William on the elevator in the new part of the old hospital, hotel-like in its lobby, full of floors organized by fatal illnesses—oncology, neurology, infectious diseases, eye, nose, and ear, and finally, cardiology. Eventually, William would find himself on every level, except oncology.

Today it was 6E—cardiology. 6E was fluorescent. Behind the nurses' station, a white-board schedule hung above rows of infants in plastic swings suspended from creaking metal. Some swinging, some running out of swing and needing cranking again. This was what the babies were there for—a recharge. The fluorescent lights, the swinging babies, the city of broken hearts—another new world William had brought me to in the short one and a half months of his life.

It was time to get down to the business of fixing William's heart. Fortunately, denial would not allow me to register how sick he was. Denial shielded me from considering that he was on the brink of death. For our entire stay in Children's Hospital, it never crossed my mind that he could die, and I thank denial for that. As I crossed the threshold into the long journey that would save William's life, everything I knew as strength flushed to the bottom of my heart and started to crawl up again. That's what crying is—something starts threatening the soul, and the hurt whirls into a ball and begins to roll out. I am well-versed in trapping hurt and pushing it back. Now, I carried a part of William's soul with me, which gave me the strength I needed to take the next step.

Signing off

William had congestive heart failure. When he was strong enough, weeks after the nurses fed him through a tube that ran down his nose into his stomach, he had his catheterization. A specialist threaded a catheter with a camera on it through William's femoral artery to take pictures of how the blood pumped and flowed through his heart.

During William's catheterization, I parked myself in a crowded waiting room with other parents of children undergoing heart surgery. It had the ambiance of a nursing home, except young parents did puzzles and looked anxious.

I went into the puzzle room thinking a mindless jigsaw might distract me, and there were few other places to sit. There was one phone in the puzzle room, and a father talked on it in muffled tones. His conversation crept into my space. He was trying to explain to his mother how his daughter had had a stroke during her catheterization. This happens. This is why I signed William's life away before surgery. This was the fine print in action.

"Yes, Mom, a stroke," he repeated. "No, Mom, she is not okay. No, she may not get better. I don't know, Mom. Mom, it happened. The doctor told me. She may be paralyzed. I know, Mom, but she may not be okay." The conversation went on and on—a son trying to explain the unexplainable to his mother.

The Fantastic Voyage

After William's catheterization, Tom arrived from New Hampshire, and Doctor Flanagan took us to see the filmstrip of how William's blood flowed through his heart. We followed him to the bowels of the hospital to watch a film with little hairs on it projected on the pale-yellow wall.

The projector click-click-clicked. The only other projectors I had encountered were in science class, where science was neat, clean, and right. And home movies where life was fairy tale memories of perfect children with perfect hearts. It was like watching *The Fantastic Voyage*, a 1966 film starring Raquel Welch, about a team of scientists traveling through another scientist's blood in a miniature submarine called Proteus. Catheterization is science fiction—a fantastic journey through the bloodstream.

What I saw before me was real, not some blurry fantasy of an amoeba or the highlights of my childhood. The yellow wall absorbed the shimmering projection of William's heart pumping in choppy sequences. It seemed to start its journey well, but William's heart only had one valve and two chambers instead of four. His one valve was four times the size it should have been, by infant standards. The blood in his heart could not make it through the aorta to nourish William with the oxygen he needed to survive. As his blood sloshed its way from one chamber of his heart to the next it found no way to escape and feed his body with oxygenated blood. His blood tried to push through his aorta but met an obstacle called a coarctation that cinches the artery keeping the blood from entering the rest of his body.

Dr. Flanagan showed us how the surgeons were going to make it right. William would undergo two operations. First, they would repair the coarctation in William's aorta. If they fixed his valve first, his aorta wouldn't be able to handle the massive flow of blood coming from his broken heart.

The aorta procedure was a simple cut and paste. The surgeon would cut out the coarctation and then sew Will's tiny artery back together. In the second surgery, the surgeons would put William on a by-pass machine to divert the blood from his heart like a tributary, open his heart and divide his one valve into four pieces. Then, they would use a snippet of Gore-Tex to provide an anchor upon which to build four chambers in his heart. (Dr. Gore invented Gore-Tex for this purpose before Gore-Tex became rain gear material guaranteed to keep wetness out.)

After watching the film, I understood William's exhaustion. I knew how the heart should work, and the film showed me how William's didn't work. William's heart was fighting with all of its might for his life. William began his life with the determination to live even if it meant beating the odds.

The Wait

William's aorta was repaired quickly. I was so focused on the open-heart surgery this repair seemed almost insignificant, but I am reminded of it every time I see the C-shaped scar that curves from his chest, under his arm and to the center of his back.

What followed was a long wait. I had been a student at Boston University and had trained for the Lightweight Women's National Rowing Team on the Charles River in the early eighties. I had coached the Northeastern University Novice Crew there as well, so friends of mine were spread throughout the city. People visited me every day. Sometimes they gave me reprieve to go for a long run along the river. Other times we chatted, and my friends held William. Some were too afraid to be left alone with William. I suppose I had become oblivious to the feeding tube, the IV, and various tubes snaking their way in and out of William's body. I never thought he was on his deathbed. It felt safe to be in Children's Hospital, but the waiting started to become unbearable.

Once, when William was scheduled for surgery, four newborns were helicoptered in for immediate, urgent operations. Each of their hearts was wired the wrong way and needed readjustment. Another time we were ready to go, William got a fever. The doctor said we could go home with him for a few days if we were careful. We ended up spending twenty-four hours in our local hospital because the intern had prescribed an overdose of antibiotics.

Babies needing immediate care streamed into Children's Hospital. The nurses were able to keep William alive, so he was the first one to get bumped. Then his surgeon went on vacation. I cracked on that one, packed William's things, and started to leave. Dr. Flanagan said, "You may leave, but William can't."

The Baby with the Rocker-Bottom Feet

William and I had many roommates on 6E at Boston Children's Hospital. William slept in the hospital crib. I got the pull-out couch. Sometimes we had one roommate; other times, we had up to eight. I remember one well.

This boy was William's age, about one-month-old, and he had rocker-bottom feet. He had Edward's Syndrome, which is the second most common autosomal trisomy among live-born children, Trisomy-21 being the first.

A thin privacy curtain dangling from a strip of metal hooks separated us from him. William and I had the window side this time, with all the sunlight and a spectacular view of the city. Our roommate lay on the dark side of the room. Alone, he cried all the time. His cry was telling me something, but I wasn't listening.

What kind of mother wouldn't be with her baby? How could this mother not be here for him? *I* said that to someone who was visiting us. *Me*, who had planned the date of William's birth to fall at the end of midwinter break so I could take a paid maternity leave for the next six months. Boy, did I have a lesson to learn.

The curtain separating us from the baby with the rocker bottom feet opened in a cacophonous clatter and swayed against the wall. Light from our side of the room shed onto the nurse tending to our roommate. How dare you, she didn't say, but her glare stabbed my words.

Then the nurse told me why the baby with the rocker bottom feet was alone. Icicles dripped off of every word. Where was my compassion for the single mother of this child? A mother who had two other children she could not afford to leave home. Where was my empathy for a woman who couldn't take time off from her job, which may or may not have been enough to pay the rent each month? My lack of humility rendered me speechless for a long time—this is the first time I have spoken of it.

I never met this boy's mother. I don't know what happened to the baby with rocker bottom feet—if he made it or not. He taught me a lesson—one I should adhere to every day as I stumble through my life. I was guilty of making a sweeping judgment and assuming his mother was negligent. I can't imagine what it would have been like to leave William alone in a hospital crib in Boston so I could continue working and ensuring the rest of my childrens' well-being.

Was he coming back?

After I held you
before you disappeared through the double doors,
they swaddled you in a warm blanket.
The heat,
your frail body,
like an angel with a broken wing,
leaked into my chest.
After they gathered you,
their sheer shower caps
bobbed like dandelions
through double doors.
The smooth swish of foot covers
slipped soundlessly away.

Trust

There is no definitive day or night in the hospital. Things happen when they happen. It was early morning when the team prepped William and said he was ready to go. But was I? I had held William the night before. I didn't know how I could ever let him go into the hands of surgeons who were going to open his heart. Where was the guarantee he would come back alive? The anesthesiologist had me sign a form to ensure that if William died, I wouldn't blame anyone. The fine print said more than I wanted to read about the risks I was taking by sending him into the operating room.

"What would happen if I didn't sign?" I let this ridiculous question slip from my lips.

"We would make him a ward of the state and have them sign it."

I sat in a chair with William and cried, which the anesthesiologist couldn't handle, so he called a nurse to deal with me. William was too young, weak, and inexperienced to fear what was coming, so I felt it for him. The nurse pulled a warm blanket out of a blanket heater, and its warmth let me release William into her arms.

After William disappeared beyond the double doors, I found myself alone in another waiting room. The room was as packed as the catheterization waiting room, but it was in the new part of the hospital—clean, white, and optimistic. There was a mixed crowd. Some children waited for out-patient surgery, but mostly, parents waited for their children coming out of various operations. An eight-year-old boy was anticipating a circumcision. I resisted asking his father why he hadn't done it when he was born. I was glad I hadn't put William through that extra pain.

The nurse gave us a beeper so we would know when William's operation was over or if they needed us to come back if there were any complications. A nurse in the operating room could give us a blow by blow account of each stage of William's operation. I didn't want to stay for that. It wasn't as if I could do anything for William now anyway.

As I was deciding to go outside and sit in the sun, my friend Swift Corwin lumbered down the hall. He is a forester, a lumberjack, by profession. He towered over everyone else in the room and brought with him a sense of reality and relief. The world had still turned while William and I were living at Children's. Swift knew William was in Children's Hospital, but there was no way he could have known William was in surgery that day. We hadn't told anyone because we were so used his getting bumped, but there was Swift as if he had walked straight out of the New Hampshire woods he forested for a living.

May Magnolias

May spread its magnolia wings
to wrap me in its warm cocoon
That May magnolia day
a friend swept in
floating like his name—
Swift
like Cupid with his arrow
spreading the heat of the magnolia's bloom,
the sun,
and a blanket warming my hope.

Beeps, Bypasses, and Basking

Basking in the sun with Swift and Tom, I picked neatly trimmed blades of grass off the Harvard Medical School Quad. It didn't matter what we said. I stuffed my anxiety inside the lump in my stomach as we all dodged the fear we felt but were afraid to express. Tom and Swift passed the time talking about I don't know what.

During the month and a half in the hospital, I was hyper-focused on William. I couldn't talk or think about anything else because if I did, I would let something in that might jinx or curse the whole medical process. I couldn't think about anything but William's well-being. All of this time, I kept shark eyes on William, insisting that people wash their hands before they touched him, guarding against the occasional person who wandered into the hospital from the street to pray for him. One false move on my part, even a thought, could put William in danger.

I was also protecting myself from letting my doubts about our future flood my mind. At Children's Hospital, I shut out the rest of the world grateful it couldn't get in. I had no doubt about William's survival, but this was the first time I had let him out of my sight and trusted the doctors to take care of him.

The beeper beckoned us three hours later. The surgery was over sooner than we thought. I didn't know what was next in this process. When Tom and I got to the surgical floor, William's four surgeons walked toward me like giants in matching blue. How could men with such big hands fix William's, infantile-fist-sized heart? The first thing the primary surgeon said was, "He gave us a bit of trouble getting off of the heart-lung machine, but he pulled himself through." Those are the only words I exchanged with the man who saved my son's life. I will always wonder how close William came to the edge and what brought him back.

In post-op, William looked suspended from where he lay. The medical staff used morphine to spare him the pain of feeling anything after such invasive surgery. Tubes of all sizes slithered in his body and sucked out the liquids that could endanger his recovery. A scar zipped his chest with a combination of his blood and liquid glue to spare him the railroad track scars people used to get with open-heart surgery. The two half-inch rubber chest tubes on either side of his chest leaked a pus-like liquid into a square see-through box at the end of his bed. Wires dangled out from his heart in case it stopped and needed a jump start. A tube, corrugated like a vacuum cleaner hose, went straight to his lungs and breathed for him. Beepers beeped for him, and those surrounding him. It would take some time before he would look alive.

It took an agonizing hour for the nurses to get William situated in the ICU. When they let us in to see him again, he was awake, but the staff had to keep him on the ventilator because his oxygen levels weren't right. He cried frantically, defenselessly. There was nothing to do about it beyond wrenching out the ventilator myself. After all, he was crying—a sure sign he was breathing. This moment was the hardest one I have faced in William's lifetime, and I couldn't hold him, touch him, or be there for him. The staff surrounded him, and there was no room for me to squeeze into the fray. I couldn't watch him suffer, so I left.

The surgical nurse called us back minutes later. William was sleepy and still suspended in after-surgery bliss minus the ventilator. He stayed in ICU for a few days until they released him into an in-between ICU space. He was on 6E again with a roommate, and a nurse stayed with them around the clock.

One More Thing

Tom and I were exhausted. William had made it through the worst of it. So, leaving him under a nurse's care, we went to a friend's apartment to take a nap. Two hours later, we arrived to see William in a soaked diaper, and no nurse or roommate was in sight. There were severe complications with the roommate, so William's assigned nurse had left him on his own.

I worried about the neglect, so I changed his diaper, and another nurse let me hold him for the first time since he had left me for surgery. For a moment, I cradled William, whose pre-surgery grey cheeks were a new pink, then I noticed his eyes darting once to the left of his sockets. "Something is wrong," I said. I could sense it in the brief seconds William's eyes rolled to the left. The nurse grabbed him and ordered me out of the room.

William had had a seizure. Seizures of all degrees happen to people after heart surgery, and William's minor seizure was almost insignificant. Still, he had to undergo an electroencephalogram (EEG) to rule out epilepsy. I had been so focused on his heart. I hadn't considered that anything would happen after the surgery. The neurologist didn't rule out epilepsy, so, erring on the side of caution, he added anti-seizure medicine to the litany of other drugs William was already taking for his recovery.

William returned to the general population on 6E two days later, where people were either waiting for surgery or reaching the end of the surgical road. Now William was pink and not blue. He looked brand new. When I fed him a two-ounce bottle of formula, he sucked it down without any effort. That was the final test.

Elevating into the Real World

And then, almost suddenly, William was well enough to go home. I didn't want to go. Children's Hospital had sheltered me as much as my son. I didn't need to explain William to people who didn't know what to say. I had lived in a separate world where people helped me take care of him. I didn't have to make medical assumptions, and they took care of my worry. Plus, there were so many other parents of children with Trisomy-21 there. Now I would be on my own. Tom would be working, and I found myself growing apart from him as I centered everything on William instead.

I rewound my way out of the hospital. Past the babies swinging beneath the surgery schedule at the nurses' station. Past the squeak of the swings that needed rewinding. Down the fluorescent hallway and to the elevator. William shuddered as our guts slid up with the downward motion of the elevator and for me lodging the lump in my throat. To this day, he reminds me of that elevator ride, when he presses his body to a corner of an elevator and braces himself as he elevates up or down.

Denial

I found out that William could have died after he didn't die. Denial kept that thought from crossing my radar until a year later when William was a plump, thriving, non-toddling toddler. To me, William had never been *that* sick. Everyone else's babies were *that* sick—their babies were transparent from their heart defects, but not mine. In the eight weeks William and I spent at Children's Hospital, I had never feared for his life.

One year after William's surgery, I met a family whose son had the same heart condition William had had. "Look at William," I said. "He used to be like your son"—I had never noticed how gaunt and gray William had been before his heart surgery. I told them their son was going to have a repeat experience of the one William had. Then they could get back to a life free of doctors, blood tests, and sleepless nights. I never thought I was wrong to reassure them and give them hope. I wanted to ease their fears and pass down all I had learned to make their journey less horrific than mine. But just as every person is not the same, so surgery is not the same.

I never saw this family again. I heard through the Trisomy-21 grape-vine their son did not make it through the surgery. Only then did I grasp how close William had come to the same fate. My denial had protected me from this thought for those six weeks.

Trying to Rise

With our hospital days over and two months left of my maternity leave, William and I settled into a routine of long runs with William tucked into his baby jogger, lots of tea, and the treasure of a healthy child. William grew. It felt as if we were starting his life again.

RISE sent a physical or occupational therapist or social worker to our house to bounce William on bouncy balls, reach for toys with one hand and then the next, to track with his eyes, sit up, crawl, talk, and walk. They tried their hardest, and so did I, to encourage William to develop. Looking back on those days, the therapist and I did most of the work, and William tolerated it. It wasn't much fun, but it was reassuring to have someone from the outside understand his setbacks and accomplishments, which might seem insignificant to others. William's development never caught up with those of his peers. Everyone knew it, but Early Intervention was supposed to increase progress in their clients, and they were not about to give up.

On the days RISE didn't come to our house, William and I dabbled in lake water, soaked in the sun, and started life over again now that he had the heart to do so. At one year, he still didn't crawl on all fours. He communicated with sign language and engaged in some of the multitudes of toys in which I almost drowned him. I imagined the excessive stimulation RISE recommended would change William's lot in life and turn him into someone whose Trisomy-21 was not the first thing that people saw when they met him.

At first, I was obsessed with the mission to do everything I could to enhance those crucial years of his cognitive growth. While other mothers marked their baby books and boasted as their children rolled over, got new teeth, or uttered something sounding like Mama, William signed Mama with his tiny fingers.

If I could do it all over again, I wouldn't take the same approach to his cognitive growth. I would let William develop on his terms, which he did anyway. RISE and I were the ones trying to make him catch up to other kids his age. Part of me doubted all of this intervention was necessary, but what if I was wrong? I didn't trust my intuition, which is always a big mistake.

Children read when they read, talk when they talk, and walk when they feel ready to do so. Public school systems regulate what age a child should develop, but most children determine the rate they will accomplish these milestones. In the end, most children will walk or find a way to get around, talk or discover another means to communicate, and read in some fashion, whether it is with pictures or words.

William developed at his own pace. I am not sure if our early intervention gyrations made any difference, and I will never know. Eventually, William walked at age five, used sign language intermittently, and spoke in a way that his family and close friends could understand.

Total Communication

When he was two, William participated in Elizabeth Gibb's Total Communication study. A speech therapist selected a group of toddlers with Trisomy-21 who didn't talk yet. She wanted to prove sign language, and other means of non-verbal communication for toddlers with delays in language eased their frustration and improved their communication skills. The case study revealed there was little to no effect on comprehension, but many of the toddlers in the group made significant gains in their language.

A speech therapist came to our house and played with William once a week. She introduced 20 new verbal words with total communication through play. The therapist lay the foreground for how I could learn to respect and understand William's words through my questions, his gestures, and a lot of patience. I learned to encourage William to point at something to show me or hint to me what he was trying to tell me. I could ask him to say something in a different way, or to give us a clue using a sign. This provided William with a transition process to become more verbal. It also gave him and those close to him a means to communicate for the rest of his life.

My obsession with early intervention started to fade. I may have been as bored by it as William was. Mainly, it wore off because he was becoming someone with a big personality, which brought William and me more joy than any toy he reached for or any ball he bounced on.

One day while William and I were roughhousing, I noticed he had grown two bottom teeth. I am not sure what I expected, but when I saw those faded pieces of calcium pushing through his gum, I couldn't believe it. He had a tooth! William had something other kids had! I was so busy looking at the big picture of his life, that I forgot that one day he might lose a tooth, grow, stand, walk, and get through toilet training like every other kid.

On another sunny morning, William and I lolled on the soft, pink rug in his room, ignoring his early intervention toys. Then, he laughed for the first time. A chortle slipped out of his lips. I wasn't sure. I rolled onto my back, pulled him onto my belly, lifted him into the air, and jostled another laugh out of him. He laughed again. We spent the afternoon laughing and exploding with joy and delight. He had laughter, which was all he needed—his infectious laugh has carried him far.

Rebirth

During the summer after William's surgery, as I was settling into the next phase of William's life, I went to an event called Up with Down's—an unnerving turn of phrase for a new mother who has just been to Hell and back after learning her plane landed in Holland. A mother who couldn't nurse her first newborn because he had a heart defect and didn't have the strength to eat. A mother who learned her son had the heart defect typical in fifty percent of children with Trisomy-21. He also had an aorta in need of repair, which is not so common in infants with Trisomy-21. Even though I was not feeling "up with Downs," I needed to learn what other parents were doing now that William was well.

I have always shied away from group gatherings like these, preferring to bond with people as they meandered into my life. But the "I shoulds" started to arise when William and I returned from our stint at Children's Hospital. My "I should" voice told me I had to join the Trisomy-21 culture. Up with Downs was the first event that came up, so I forced myself to go, and I dragged William and Tom along with me.

Up with Downs is an advocacy group associated with the Trisomy-21 community. I don't mean to downplay their mission to improve the lives of people with Trisomy-21. I applaud it. It brings an awareness to people that having a child with Trisomy-21 is a positive and not a negative as "Down syndrome" suggests.

Up with Downs tells people who don't understand Trisomy-21 that having a child with it is uplifting because he or she is as beautiful as any other child could be. For that, I appreciate their message. Up with Downs is for the general population, people who look at Trisomy-21 as a curse, which it isn't.

I am not keen on clichés, and this turn of phrase irked me because it felt fake—as if people were trying too hard to make the best of it when it's easier to evolve with the situation and admit it's hard. I still struggled. Having a son with Trisomy-21 is a rough journey, no matter how much we love and accept our children. Paving the road for someone with Trisomy-21means being overwhelmed by government agencies, early intervention, and school and medical systems, which are close to impossible to understand if you try to use common sense.

Sometimes I felt like Job in the Old Testament who was given one impossible test after another to prove his faith to God. Faith in God has never been my forte, but someone or something was putting me to the test. I thought Up with Downs might give me some strength or introduce me to someone with whom I could connect. I wasn't going there because I had an inkling it would. I was going because I was picking at straws to find my way forward. I made it through the hard parts of heart surgery. I was starting to adjust to Holland and learning how to be a parent. Up with Downs seemed like an appropriate step deeper into the world of Trisomy-21.

When I went to the Up with Downs picnic, it was too soon in my journey to embrace it. I loved William, but I was still wallowing in my victimhood. I couldn't, and still can't, believe that everything about Downs is up. Life has its peaks and valleys. When you reach a peak, you feel high. When you hit bottom, it's a challenge to climb back up to the summit.

Eventually, I came to see the upside to Trisomy-21. As William and I grew together and laughed together, he brought our community alive with all of the caring and love they shared with us. The upside of Trisomy-21 grew exponentially. It was William who pulled me up.

Convention

The next group experience I signed up for was not a cliché. William, Tom, and I went to the National Down Syndrome Convention in Boston when William was less than a year old. We met up with our old hospital friends—Nathan and William had both had open heart surgery at the same time.

Every year the National Down Syndrome Congress holds a convention of experts to talk about Trisomy-21—doctors, specialists, behaviorists, and estate planners who knew how to set up a special needs trust so state and federal money wouldn't get taken away. The people attending share the experience of raising someone with Trisomy-21. We went there to learn all we could about the journey before us.

Going to the Down Syndrome Convention, meant entering our separate culture for a day. Everyone either had Trisomy-21 or was connected to it through family, friendship, or curiosity. It was different from the Up with Down's event because it laid out the facts and the reality of a world new to many of us there—a culture where no one did a double-take when William spoke, flapped his hands, used his army crawl to get around, or was who he was. It was a culture where we were not unique because we had a son with Trisomy-21. Everyone there shared this cool, comfortable secret about living life with a child who had Trisomy-21.

I am breaking all the rules by advocating we be homogeneous every once in a while, but there are times when it feels comforting to settle in with your own kind. It's like coming home to your family. What is heterogeneity anyway? Who defines it? Can culture be homogeneous if the sameness is that we are all human?

Many novice parents wanted to hear from siblings about their experience growing up with a brother or sister with Trisomy-21. The panel appeared awkward and a little put upon. Finally, one of them piped up, "These questions about how they affected our lives are tough to answer because we don't know what it is like not to have a sibling with Trisomy-21." Today, Kate and Claire have the same reaction when I ask them what I should say about what it was like for you growing up with William.

Claire says, "I hate it when people ask me that. What am I supposed to say? I don't know what it would have been like to grow up without him."

Educators, specialists, and pediatricians told me that William's siblings would help him to develop faster. Faster than what? I thought he might teach his younger sisters more than I ever would. Would they learn patience and acceptance? Would they accept his differences? I can't answer these questions because they never had a preconceived notion of who William was *supposed* to be.

In his first year, William had taught me that things take time to evolve, and that timing doesn't always matter. Too often, I fill the blank spaces of my life with fear instead of mindfulness. I sometimes feel that if my life isn't brimming over, the burn of emptiness might destroy me. As a teacher, my life has been a series of nine-week increments with intermittent splits for vacations. My days had become a series of ticks on the calendar. William pulls me back and shows me the shortfalls of my pace. He is a constant reminder to slow down and pay attention to the details of life, to walk two steps slower than everyone else. It doesn't matter who gets there first.

He continues to show me that each of us learns and grows in our way no matter what society deems appropriate. William gives me this knowledge. If his first year was any indication of his future, then he chose to be brave, resilient, compassionate, with a strong will to laugh and live.

Playing Defense

In William's early years, I was defensive about the comments people made about him. I didn't recognize that much of their concern was for me. I translated, "I am sorry for your suffering" into a personal affront about Trisomy-21.

When people mentioned my suffering, I would spit back, "people with Trisomy-21 don't suffer. It is not a disease." When people suggested how hard this must be for me, I bristled at the thought. The truth is that it was hard. I *did* struggle against doctors, medical, governmental, and school bureaucracy, and the social mores that come with a child who has Trisomy-21. Defending myself was a way of protecting my fear. If I let on to myself that this challenge was as big as it was, it might have overwhelmed me. So I battened down the hatches and forged ahead.

On the other hand, it felt as if people thought something horrible happened to me because William was born. I stewed about this, but I kept it to myself. Was there something so wrong with William he was deserving of these statements? As I grew with William, and in hindsight, I recognized my confrontational approach toward people who said, or say the wrong thing. They were as new to this as I was.

But I wished that more people had the common sense to think about what they were saying to me. I wanted someone else to understand how it felt to be me. On the flip side, I didn't let anyone in to show them how I felt, because I felt guilty about the doubts I had about being William's mother. My need for help and understanding and my natural tendency to have a stiff upper lip polarized me. I didn't have the sense to tell people how their words made me feel.

I have tried to train myself over the years to stop before I speak, to contemplate, and then correct someone who gets things wrong. It is a discipline I may not have learned if William hadn't come along. Now, I try to moderate my own words to make sure I don't do the same things, but I am not always so successful.

William *isn't* the same as all of *those* "Down syndrome children." He is his unique self, and besides, people need to know not to precede *children* with "Down syndrome" because the disability doesn't come first. William has Trisomy-21. He is not a Down syndrome person. He is a person who has Down syndrome.

It takes time for people to understand that Trisomy-21 is not a disease. People don't suffer from it. You can't catch it or get it from contaminated food or water. Trisomy-21 is a genetic anomaly. Scientists still don't know what causes the nondisjunction in cells when chromosomes do not divide correctly in utero, as is the case with Trisomy-21. There is no evidence supporting that environmental factors have anything to do with it. It is genetic, not hereditary.

There are days when I cannot hold myself back if someone confuses William with another person, or someone else asks me, "How long will he live?" In response to my scowl, "I mean Down syndrome people die early. Right?" Not necessarily. This generation of individuals who have Trisomy-21 is the first generation to have heart surgery to cure their congenital heart defect, instead of leaving them to die. It is also the first generation who lived under the Individuals with Disabilities Act (IDEA), which allows people with different abilities to go to public school.

I want William to be the one to squash the mortality myth. My cousin Suzie is 63-years-old and as healthy as can be. Unfortunately, William isn't Suzie. He falls into the 50% who have heart defects. When he was little, I knew that heart repair would come back to haunt us. At this point, I was keeping my personal questions about his mortality at bay.

As far as the mortality rate question is concerned, there is nothing kind about asking that question.

Shower Thoughts

Trisomy-21 is a chance event. One in 700 mothers in the United States has a William at the center of their universe. William was born to me because I needed him more than most people do—because there was so much about life that I didn't know. I had lived my life in a cloud of not understanding, feeling disconnected, and out of sorts with the world. When I slipped into depression, it was dark and murky. I had no idea what depression was, but I knew that there was something wrong with me.

I was raised in a culture that segregated people with differences. In the generation before me, doctors told mothers like my Aunt Phoebe, Suzie's mother, to give up a child with Trisomy-21. When William was born, I needed to unwrap my wrapping paper to find something bright and precious. I don't mean to say I deserve special privileges, but I got one in William. I didn't understand this the day he was born thirty years ago.

When I hurdled the obstacles I faced for William, I was not about to fall apart in public. I wouldn't show how I was coming apart inside. What kind of person would that make me? One who doesn't want her child? These were my shower thoughts. In the shower, the tears streamed down my body with the scalding hot water. They didn't streak my face and become a separate part of me. In the shower, my tears didn't leak. They flowed. No one else saw them.

Birth, Life, or Choice?

When I became pregnant with Kate soon after William returned from the hospital, Tom and I decided I should have an amniocentesis. Not because we would abort or because the odds of having another child with Trisomy-21 was likely. We already knew everything we needed to know about genetics, and what it meant to have a baby with Trisomy-21. But we wanted to be ready just in case, so we opted for an amniocentesis, which requires counseling.

We packed William into the car and drove to Boston for the recommended counseling about amniocentesis. Most people have an amniocentesis to see if their child has a disability. Some abort when they find out, some don't.

I am not sure how many clients bring their babies who have Trisomy-21 to sessions as we did for pre-amniocentesis counseling sessions like these, but I didn't think of the irony of it until I saw the counselor's mouth drop when I took William out of his snuggly to reveal my swollen belly that carried Kate.

From my experience, the assumption in the medical world is that parents will abort when they find out that their child has an abnormality. I had confirmed this a year before when I went to see my obstetrician for my six-week post checkup with William. The obstetrician said, "Did you have amniocentesis?"

"No," I replied, not wanting to hear what was coming next.

"Well, we won't let that happen again, will we?"

I looked down at William that day and thought loudly, "That's right because I am never going to come back here again.

Choice

Once, a friend told me her daughter-in-law was carrying a child with Trisomy-21. My friend wanted to talk with me to prepare—she had already named the child. She wanted to know what to expect. How could she be the best grandmother? What was the best support she could give? Then she mentioned her son and daughter-in-law were not sure if they were going to keep the baby. They were weighing their options. They hadn't made the choice.

I couldn't introduce them to William or help them decide whether or not to bring their child to term. They were too far away. Besides, I remembered how hard it was for me when William was born, to meet older people with Trisomy-21 because it forced me to face the future when I wasn't ready to face the present. I couldn't share the challenges and the joys of raising him. I couldn't share my wisdom. I couldn't sway them one way or the other. I could only share my friend's joy at the prospect of having a grandson, who also had an extra chromosome.

I believe in choice. Yes, there is a giant BUT in there. I didn't know William had Trisomy-21 when he was in utero. I am grateful I didn't because, what if, in my ignorance, I had chosen to abort William?

I had not heard from this friend for a long time. When I ran into her at the recycling center, I already sensed what her son and his wife had decided, but I asked anyway to make it real. When she confirmed their choice, I didn't begrudge them for their decision to abort. It's not my place. People have the right to make their choice. It was a loss—the profound loss of something so precious that they and the world will never know.

Sam

Three years after William was born, I was four and a half months pregnant with my third child, Sam. I agreed to have amniocentisis because I couldn't decide, so I left my decision to Tom, even though my gut told me not to. There are as many reasons to have amniocentesis as there aren't, which is why I was ambivalent.

One advantage of having an amniocentesis is it can forewarn you of the maze of knowledge you need to navigate when you have a child with Trisomy-21. You can do further tests to see if your child has a heart defect. You can find an early intervention program. You can familiarize yourself with the bureaucratic systems you will need to receive help from them, no matter how difficult they make it for you to do so. You can also find a whole new world of people you would never know if it wasn't for your child. The most important reason for knowing your newborn has Trisomy-21 is it will let you celebrate his or her birth when the time comes rather than recovering from the shock of not knowing.

But everything about *this* amniocentesis felt wrong—the assembly line of rooms, each one with a woman lying flat on her back. Same-sized little humps waited for the doctor to go from one of us to the next with his foot-long needle to inject and draw amniotic fluid from the sacs protecting our children. Sam was alive. I saw him wiggling in the ultrasound picture. I also saw the needle going in. It must have scared him. It scared me.

The nurses swept me out of the room as quickly as they had swept me in. I rolled over to heave myself off the crinkled paper covering the table. Before I left the room, I heard the nurse ripping off the paper and bunching it into an insignificant ball, while another nurse called in the next patient. Is that what they did all day—locate the amniotic sac, insert the needle, roll the pregnant patient off the white paper, rip it off, and proceed to the next patient?

Since we were in Nashua, Tom needed to make a stop for some stereo equipment. I resented the extra time Sam and I would have to wait to get home and take care of ourselves. I lay in the back seat of the car and tried to sleep. I had wanted to be cautious about this baby, to go right home, lie down, and let him recover from something so invasive. I had taken a pillow along for the forty-five-minute drive home so Sam and I could rest together in the back seat.

I rested for the next two days. Then a friend asked me to join her for a swim. For some, a swim means a dip. For me, it could mean a three-hour swim around Lake Nubanusit. It crossed my mind as a foolish idea because it was so close to the amniocentesis, but when I thought of Sam swaying along in his amniotic fluid, through the soft water of Norway Pond, I thought it would be gentle enough for him.

The next day, I went to a prenatal check-up with Kate and William in tow. The doctor couldn't find Sam's heartbeat, so she sent me to the hospital for an ultrasound. As I lay on the starch white crinkled paper covering the examination table, my neck creaked up to see the small black and white screen showing Sam's body. Kate occupied herself with coloring a picture, and William wouldn't leave my side. He draped himself over my body—over Sam. People tried to move him away, but I needed his comfort. I urged them to let him stay right where he was. I knew Sam wasn't alive, and I knew it was my fault. I had agreed to have the amniocentesis. I had let Tom stop at the store in Nashua, and I had gone swimming. It had all been too much for Sam, and now he was dead.

I pleaded with the doctor to do the D&C right away, but it was late in the day, and I had food in my system. It had to wait until the next morning.

I drove to Willard Pond, my most sacred place, still carrying Sam's body inside of mine. I hiked out to Blueberry Point and walked knee-deep in the water and let Sam go—giving him away to nature. I was so sorry, so crushed that I had chosen the path I had.

Advice

Years later, my sister was in the first trimester of her pregnancy with her third child. A test had come back insinuating that the child could have Down syndrome. "Do you think I should have amniocentesis?" she asked.

"Would you abort your child if it had Trisomy-21?" I asked.

"Of course not!" She was surprised I asked.

"If you wouldn't abort, then don't have the amniocentesis," I advised. "There is a risk of miscarriage. The Mayo Clinic says there is a slight chance, 0.1-.0.3 percent. Even though it is small, someone has to make up that slight percentage. I did."

She heeded my advice and decided not to have the amniocentesis. I think that she just needed affirmation anyway. However, when my mother found out that I told her not to have amniocentesis, she was furious. She called me and said, "How could you tell her *not* to have one?"

"It is her choice," I responded, trying to keep from sending fatal lightning bolts across the telephone wire. "I didn't tell her what to do. I just gave her advice, Mom."

My mother never accepted William. She put up a feeble front to pretend she did, but he was an embarrassment to her. We never talked about it, but it drove a stake through our already tenuous relationship.

"What if her child has Down's?" she wasn't holding anything back.

"Mom, this is not a conversation that we are going to have," my maturity surprised me. For once, I wasn't folding under her judgment of William—her insinuation that by advising Amanda not to have amniocentesis, might mean another William.

"I have to talk about it," she snapped.

"Then talk to a therapist, because I am not going to discuss this any further with you."

My younger sister didn't have a baby with Trisomy-21. I attended the birth just because I had always wanted to see one. The first question my mother asked me after Amanda's daughter was born was, "Is the baby okay?" I handed the phone to Amanda and let her deal with it.

My mother was not a demon. However, she never did learn to embrace William and see way beyond Trisomy-21 and into his soul.

Kate

Kate met a brother whose perspective and approach to life are unique to other brothers. Since they were 12 months apart and William was not anywhere near to being ready to walk, they moved around together for the first year of Kate's life, sweeping the floor with their bellies as he showed her the army crawl. He crooked one arm in front of himself, heaved up and then over it to propel forward, like a soldier crawling under barbed wire. Kate followed suit. Soon, she learned that crawling on her hands and knees was more efficient.

Their curiosity was attached—whatever one found the other would investigate as seriously. They peered under couches together and found dust bunnies under the chair. One day they discovered the six-inch black and white TV we used for videos, turned it on, and stared at the static. Other times, I might find Kate sitting in the toy box, doling out the toys that William couldn't reach. In Kate's first year, they taught each other how to navigate the world from the belly level. He was not going to be like everyone else's brother, but that was not on Kate's mind.

Kate started to walk at around the time William graduated to his scooching method to propel himself. He stretched both crossed legs in front of himself, scooched up, and thrust himself forward on his butt, shaking our poor house.

The Boy was Prince

William was the scooch master. He scooched and shimmied across the kitchen floor at a fierce clip. His progress toward walking was slow, but he learned some tricks to keep up along the way.

During this time, I bought William a Fisher-Price record player. He spent hours wearing down the vinyl grooves and driving us to near insanity playing the same story or song until the record became so worn there were no grooves in which the needle could slip. We had a collection of LPs that we were more than willing to subject to William's destruction. I also found sets of 45s at yard sales with Disney stories on them. One of his favorite 45s was *Sleeping Beauty* with mighty Maleficent, the young boy prince, and Aurora. William listened to this so much that Kate memorized the words and could recite the story.

Soon the record was so scratched it got caught in the groove introducing the boy prince. When something else preoccupied William, the needle would get stuck on "The boy was Prince...The boy was Prince...The boy was Prince..." We got so used to this, we didn't hear it, or one of us would yell up the stairs "WIIILLL fix the record!" He would lift his butt in his cross-legged stance and land with such force that the record would skip over the scratch and continue until it reached the next groove.

Transition

William was in pre-school by the time he started to walk. He did well as long as the surfaces were smooth and flat, and someone held his hand. He transitioned from early intervention into preschool and daycare at the age of three. It was a smooth transition because William and his younger sister Kate had spent two years at in-home daycare with Jay. The school picked his pre-school for him and agreed to have the school bus drive him to Jay's after pre-school since I was still teaching full-time.

Transitions can be hard for anyone, especially me, but more so for William. Many of us shift gears without thinking. We walk into a room, sit down, grab some coffee, and get to the business of doing. We hop into the car or a bus and arrive at our destination without being mindful. Sometimes we don't remember the journey we made to get to where we were going. Unlike many of us, William sits with moments of transition. He shifts his gears deliberately.

Pre-school Conundrums

In the years to come, educators tried to cure this pause, label it with possible seizure activity, or obstinacy. It became a goal in William's Individual Education Plans to eradicate these pauses. It became a problem to fix. When William learned to say NO, he used it to buy him some time.

In pre-school, William did not hang up his coat, take off his shoes and mittens, and tuck them away in his cubicle when he got off the bus—a pre-school-101 requirement. In a quandary, his team—a social worker, special educator, teacher, and aide—called in a behavioral specialist.

Most of the behavioral specialists who worked with William were cookie-cutter specialists. However, there was one behaviorist who knew his stuff. He came to William's pre-school in the morning to observe him when he got off the bus and threw his clothes on the floor. Later in his evaluation, the behaviorist told the team William did not have a behavior problem. Instead, he rewound the morning and narrated it from William's perspective.

The first thing William did in the morning, once he woke up, dressed, and ate, was to wait for the bus. When it came, Tom carried him to it because stairs and uneven surfaces were difficult for William to maneuver. It was better to carry him through this transition and sacrifice an opportunity for him to practice walking, which would have taken forever. Then, the bus driver buckled William into his car seat, and off they went. William fell asleep on his fifteen-minute drive to pre-school.

When he got to pre-school, the bus driver helped him out of his seat. Then, William had to crawl backwards down the steep bus stairs. His aide held his two hands as he practiced walking over the uneven gravel surface to the curb. The curb was a challenge. But with help, William managed to step up as a toddler does with someone holding his hands above his head and guiding him through the motion. Before he got to the door, he had to make it up three steps. Once he got through the door, his teacher expected him to hang up his coat, take off his shoes, mittens, and hat, and place them in his cubby.

The behaviorist pointed out how William's day started long before he got off the bus. He had made at least ten transitions between waking up and getting to school! The pre-school teacher's fresh beginning was near the end for William. He needed a break. And take a break he did. He plunked down, threw off his jacket, and said, "No!"

In this case, no did not mean yes. William was not ready. The remedy? The behavior plan? Let William throw his coat on the floor. Let him chill for a while. When there was a break, he could go back to his coat, hang it up, and continue with the rest of his day.

It takes a wise person to guide you along a puzzling path. This behavioral specialist wasn't a rocket scientist. He was a man with a watchful eye who reminded us to see things from William's perspective. William needed the time to focus on each detailed step along the way as everyone rushed around him to get him to school.

William had a seventh sense when it came to deciding with whom he would or wouldn't work. He took his first impression of people seriously. Unfortunately, this did not always bode well when it came to his teachers and therapists. When William clicked with someone, he was compliant. When he didn't, the teacher or therapist tried to ply him with rewards. William responds well to self-fulfilling rewards like skiing a slope without tethers, riding a horse, or planting a garden. But sometimes the rewards teachers and therapists offered him added to the agony of the original task.

Getting an unfulfilling reward for what other people wanted from him has never been worth it.

From the age of three to twenty-one, William had different aides to help him through the day. His aide was the linch-pin on his team of special educators because he or she was by William's side for the entire day, including bathroom breaks. William's aides were essential to me if they were the right fit for William, and most of them were. The aides who fit his bill were patient and loyal. They also gave me the inside scoop about what William was up to at school.

William's first experience with his pre-school aide didn't bode so well. She wore plastic gloves when she worked with him. Why I did not take that as a signal is beyond me. He didn't like her much, so he teased her and pretended he was going to spit at her by saying, "t-t." Most people he knew had a sign for their names. His aide's sign was two fingers, the H sign, gliding from William's temple to chin. William accentuated his sign with his imitation spit sound. Not so appropriate, but an accurate expression of how he felt about her. Eventually, that aide faded away. The next one didn't wear gloves or put up with William's teasing. He was okay with that.

Language, Food, and Rabbits

William was still part of the Total Communication Project. Part of William's lack of speech has to do with the size of his mouth, his low tone, his tongue, his teeth, the sensations he felt, and those he doesn't feel. Once his speech therapist rubbed an ice cube down his cheeks, and William didn't even flinch. It wasn't any wonder that he had difficulty forming words.

For most of William's early life, he ate food that was brown and round like cut up bananas, chicken nuggets, bagels, or Cheerios. When he was four, the total communication speech specialist encouraged us to expand his diet to include more challenging foods to increase the muscle tone in his mouth so he would increase the number of words he said in one sentence. At this point, he was speaking three-word sentences.

The family sat around the table at the end of a meal. Kate, Tom, and I encouraged William to eat vegetables. We knew it would be good for him, and maybe one day, he would try. We turned it into a game, knowing this change was not likely to happen any time soon. "William, do you want a carrot?"

No response.

"C'mon William try it."

"C'mon," we urged. "Just one. Try one."

We knew he wouldn't.

Then in a rare moment, William spoke in a complete sentence, head bowed, a grin on his face, and a voice loud and deep.

"I am not a rabbit."

Hope, Joy, and Concern

I used to take William and Kate to the Unitarian Universalist Church. Every Sunday, members of the church lit a candle to share hopes, joys, or concerns. One day, as the congregation proceeded to the next order of service, a man made his way to the microphone. He, like William, took a little longer to get places. His companion was able to halt the service to give the man a chance to share his concern. When this man reached the microphone, he talked about his mother, how much he loved her and missed her, and how he believed she was still with him.

This man punctured my tear bag. I wept in the front pew of the church for the remainder of the service. I imagined William without me, not understanding, the world not understanding him, alone, defenseless. A William without me. I knew Kate would fly off to college and disappear into the adult world. That is what I was raising her to do. But for William, my first child, I did not know where, when, how, or if he would fly. I had no sense of where he would be when I died. I could only imagine the now.

Star of Wonder

I still have the star. It has red felt layered with another yellow star sprinkled with gold sequins, and it was once attached to a stick. Now the felt is wrinkled and stained. The stick William once held high broke long ago. When I returned from one of my journeys and sifted through my small pile of belongings, I unearthed the star of Bethlehem William once carried in the Christmas pageant at the Unitarian Universalist Church.

In Christmas pageants, most parents display their children like stars, and each one of them twinkles brighter than all of the others. However, on pageant day, a snowstorm sabotaged my intention to get to the church early enough to make William shine.

It was a beautiful day, and the roads were slick with slush. I came to the lethal part of Route 202, where if there was going to be an accident on a snowy day, this was where it would happen. A line of cars slid to the kind of stop that always freezes the blood in my veins. Aside from the dread of bashing into someone's rear fender, stopping would make me late. To avoid further delay and the tension of waiting in a line of cars on a slush-covered highway, I detoured onto a precarious dirt road. I didn't have the patience for New Hampshire—

the snow, winter's beauty that day. In his car seat behind me, sat the Star of Wonder, and he was *not* going to miss his opportunity to shine.

I slid into the church parking lot and reached the sanctuary in time to line up for the meager procession of three kings, an ox and ass, Mary and Joseph, some sheep with curly horns, and a tangle of angels' wings. As the organ blasted Christmas carols above us, we savored the wonder of a baby's birth, the angel's call, and the star lighting the way to see this miracle. A couple from the congregation gathered around the makeshift manger followed by goats, sheep, horses, and other animals wearing costumes from Christmas pageants past.

Meanwhile, there were shepherds out in the countryside watching their flocks…

The reader continued, while a train of distracted shepherds of all ages proceeded down the aisle with shepherd sheets tied to their heads by their fathers' ties.

…then an angel stood before them.

Angel girls with wire wings, tutus, and white robes fluttered down the aisle behind the shepherds.

A child's voice echoed from the microphone—

Fear not, for I am bringing you good news of great joy for all people. To you is born this day in the city of David, a child of hope. Let this be a sign to you.

This was William's cue. He couldn't walk steadily yet, so I carried him down the aisle. He waved his wand and guided the wise men bearing their frankincense and myrrh to the manger. We stood at the altar, holding Christmas spirit in William's star.

The Christmas story tells the birth of someone who tried to make this world a better place, and on this night, I was holding the boy with the star who brought this message to this small congregation surrounding us. I watched the three wise men offer their gifts to the plastic babe in the manger. My heart was full of the warmth this community had to offer, and I wondered at the star I held—my guiding light.

Surviving

When Will and Kate were born, I planned to have them the day before February vacation so that I could include that and three months of summer vacation in my leave. Fortunately, for me, William and Kate had the same due date a year apart. However, after I miscarried Sam, I threw caution to the wind and didn't care when I got pregnant. I was going to take enough time off to be with Claire, our new baby, through her toddlerhood and to be waiting for William and Kate when they returned from first grade and kindergarten.

I told Tom I didn't want to be the breadwinner anymore—*not* a sound economic decision because my work was steady, and I had a teacher's insurance, which made the challenge of being a teacher worth it at times. On the last day of the Goodhue vacation, when I asked Tom about the logistics of his new job, I found out that he did not have a new job waiting for him when we got back. I stuck to my guns. I wanted to be a full-time mother. I deserved this time, and so did my children.

We had always struggled financially. Until then, we had been living from pay-check to pay-check, and Tom struggled to hold onto a job. I taught high school English Language Arts, but teachers do not make enough money to support a family. Teaching, lesson planning, keeping up with appointments for William, nursing, keeping the house in order, paying bills we couldn't afford to pay, were distracting me from the responsibility of raising my family. I turned to WIC, Women, Infants, and Children, a federally-funded program administered by states providing resources for families in need. I used WIC to lessen the burden of the cost of food for our family. I also took the kids to community suppers as often as possible to get a free meal. Still, I was barely making ends meet.

I played the single-parent role, even though I was married, and the financial stress added to the weight of our already faltering marriage. We were living parallel lives. When I decided to marry Tom, I was 27-years-old. I married him because he made me laugh, was artistic, and athletic. I didn't take into consideration what it would be like to face challenges with him. How could I?

I am not sure Tom was aware of the toll raising three children and having a steady and emotionally challenging job took on me or how much more support I needed. I juggled bills we couldn't pay. I learned which company was the laxest about late fees. I had become the financier. It appeared I was doing a good job juggling all of these things, but I was drowning. Perhaps my superwoman façade was strong enough for Tom to think I had this. Maybe I took over entirely and didn't let him in to make decisions or step up and take over. My trust was too thin, and it poisoned our marriage. I took on the journey of parenthood alone when it came to medical decisions, financial crises, emotional support. I was on my own. My children were my solace and my love.

Chasing Hermit Crabs

My siblings, their spouses, and children went on a Goodhue-vacation, sponsored by my generous parents, to the U.S. Virgin Island of St. John. William, now five, had learned to walk on his own. However, he hated walking on anything but level indoor ground. I carried Claire, William's youngest sister, one-month-old, in the snuggly. William and I were walking down a crumbly, steep path to the beach, while the rest of the Goodhue clan galloped ahead.

I wanted to traipse down to the beach like everyone else in my family with their bouncy, physically-confident children who fell, scraped their knees, and chased hermit crabs as they pranced and prattled along with their grandparents. Kate merged with her cousins, sauntering ahead, holding her grandmother's hand.

I wanted to be with them, not dragging William down a path he didn't want to follow. William's most effective form of communication was to dig in his heels and plop down to make himself as heavy as possible. He wanted no part of the adventure I had in store for him. I am not sure who was making more of a scene—William or me. I even spat out to a passerby, "See, here is the docile, sweet, mellow, easy-going boy all kids with Down syndrome are." I used sarcasm to articulate this non-truth with concrete evidence—people with Trisomy-21 are not always so sweet, mellow, and loving. Don't get me wrong, William is all of that, but he has a stubborn side to him that drives mothers like me to say what I said.

I should have stopped myself. I should have plopped down next to William, let the hermit crabs come to us, and let the passers-by pass. But I had this thing about getting there—being somewhere else instead of where I was, so I pulled, and struggled, and puffed, and fumed. We got there, but it wasn't a stroll of which I am proud.

Would other mothers have been frustrated with their sons? Since William has Trisomy-21, I felt under scrutiny as if there were different rules for mothers of children with Trisomy-21. Is this a confession to show you what a terrible mother I was? Perhaps it is to let you stick your nose under the tent to see how I felt. My struggle wasn't about William. It was about my desire for more, always forging ahead. I resented being held back. William was the vehicle pointing this out to me.

Living the Life

Eventually, Tom found a job, which gave me the luxury to focus on my children, a luxury that so few women have. I formed a play-group for Claire, took her to an infant swimming program, read millions of stories, played games, swung all of my children on the swings hanging from the tree in our backyard, and sang songs. We laughed and built snow forts while Claire was napping, and Kate and William learned to ski. I didn't return to teaching until Claire was ready for Kindergarten, Tom had a job, and paying the bills was doable.

William's family and community gave him more than enough to make him grow in ways he wouldn't develop in school. Academics are a small portion of what makes us decent human beings, and I gave my kids a chance to grow in other ways through nature, dance, gymnastics, and no TV, so they shaped their imaginations rather than having TV shape it for them. My years as a stay-at-home-mom allowed me to do that.

What made my children great was the challenge of a ski-slope, a fall while skating on a pond surrounded by silent puffs of snow, jumping off a rope swing before it flew back to hit the rock from which they leapt, paddling in camp-gear laden canoes to remote

Spoonwood Pond for the weekend, bobbing canoes, kayaking within three feet of a loon, putting on elaborate cousin plays on a rainy afternoon, and listening to tales about Narnia, little houses on the prairie, books by Nancie Farmer, and the poetry that children's books cradle between their covers. William fell into this intuitively with his sisters.

After Claire was born, a child at the town beach asked me if this one was all right. I should have explained to him William was all right too. William is like everyone else—he happens to have Trisomy-21. I wonder if people consider William and Trisomy-21 as the same thing. They aren't.

Support Group

Ever since my Up with Downs experience, I had dodged support groups. I figured the support group for parents of children with special needs would be similar—where everyone rejoices about having kids with special needs with trite clichés and about the blessing which we have been bestowed. There is also the flipside to support groups when people drone on about their woes but have little interest in taking any action.

Raising children is no joy ride, and throwing in a bunch of doctors, specialists, early interventionists, caseworkers, IEPs, APTD (Aid for the Permanently and Totally Disabled), and a million other acronyms doesn't make it any easier. One more group was the last thing my sarcastic self needed, but I forced myself to be open-minded, so I could learn something about what the future held for William in public school. What I didn't fathom when I walked into the meeting was that I needed all the support I could get. I had three children now, William and Kate were in school, and Claire was months old.

What resulted from my going was a life-long friendship with three women. Once We made it through the six or seven weeks of what I had feared the group would be, the four of us had no desire to re-up to the next chapter of this group. We started our own group pretending to be generous by making it an open group to which no one was invited.

Our meetings were and still are hilarious. We laugh at ourselves, our kids, and the people who cannot fathom what it would be like to share the world of our children. We make up scenarios of dropping off our kids with the Special education Director and disappearing for the day. We laugh at stories about Emily's obsession with her hair, mirrors, and Tim Allen, or at Cindy and her husband who rush to open the drapes when their light-sensitive children leave for school, or when Raf pours water into the gas tank, or when William makes up inappropriate signs for some of his less respected teachers. We laugh at what only parents of children with differences can laugh about. We get angry, we cry, we problem solve, but mostly we laugh. It is a time when we can be open about ourselves and our children. We have been getting together for 30 years.

Most of us sent our children through the same public school system. Kathy was a die-hard mainstreamer. I was something in-between. Mary took an alternative route for Raf by sending him to private schools, and at one time, starting a school. Cindy's children have no cognitive challenges. They have achromatopsia, so they see colors of the spectrum in white, gray, and black tones, have reduced visual acuity, and extreme sensitivity to bright light. Cindy also sent her son to public high school, but she chose to send her daughter to Concord Academy instead.

When our children made it to high school, either we had gained enough knowledge to make it work, the teachers were superior, or we were tired of playing defense. We struggled together knowing when our children turned 21, we would have to face the daunting transition from school life to "adult services." And we helped ourselves through that unnerving process.

Cindy's daughter went from Concord Academy to college and became a defense lawyer for people with special needs. Her achromatopsia hasn't stopped her from racing in triathlons and navigating the streets of New York City. Cindy's son Ethan graduated from Curry College, lives with his sister Allie in New York City, and is still figuring out who he wants to be while he works at the Meow Cafe. Raf and Emily both live with their parents. Raf drives a car and works at the recycling center. Emily spends

ELIZABETH GOODHUE

her days with a retired teacher in a program Kathy designed including music, art, and work. Emily also goes to Plowshare twice a week.

We are four different, strong, independent women, who could all write a modified version of this book. These women are on my gratitude list every day.

The Pierce School

When William turned five, he entered the local elementary school's kindergarten at the Pierce School. In kindergarten, it doesn't matter if you read or write, walk or crawl, speak or not speak. As long as you have a good sense of humor and strong social skills, you can fit in there, and William did. I breathed a sigh of relief. We could do this. William could go to public school like everyone else.

Joan Schnare was the teaching principal at the Pierce Elementary School. She had a thick New Hampshire accent to complement her easy smile and confident demeanor. She spoke William's language, as well. Joan embodied the concept of community. For her, William personified this spirit, and she knew how to make him feel like he did. Every time I saw Joan, she mentioned Horse Power. It took a while for me to understand what "hoss pa" meant until it caught up to the conversation.

William had started Horse Power when he was three. To say Horse Power is a therapeutic program diminishes what it is. Horse Power touches people spiritually, emotionally, psychologically, and physically. It resides on a vast, beautiful farm, with stately horses of all shapes, colors, ages, and temperaments. Everyone there moves to the smell and the rhythm of the place.

William rode Cougar once a week. It was a stretch for his short legs to reach the stirrups cinched at their highest. He looked so tiny atop such a great tender beast. William became their poster child. Years later, my brother-in-law found William's picture in a magazine. William was three years old, astride Cougar, hands outstretched, and had a smile as big as a rainbow. He and Cougar rode in horse shows. William waved to the crowds, pretending to be Curly in *Oklahoma*.

One hot day, William and Cougar waited in the middle of the ring to receive their medal after a show. Finally, Cougar had had enough. He went down to take a rest. First, his front legs buckled to the ground then his back legs followed as he rolled onto his side with William on his back. It was hot. What else was he to do? William didn't mind the excuse to leave, and neither did I.

For Joan, Horse Power was special, and she wanted Williams's class to see what he was doing. One day she announced to William's class that they were going to Horse Power to watch William ride! All of the first graders, who were lucky enough to have William in their class, trooped off to The Pony Farm to see how the other half lived.

I observed from the other side of the ring, not wanting to ruin the magic of twenty-five first graders squirming and settling in to watch their classmate do something many of them would never do. I can't tell you how William felt about this. He doesn't articulate those kinds of things. If I was to surmise from his expression, William was brimming with confidence and joy. William doesn't need words to emanate his compassion, satisfaction, pride, empathy, and feelings. That day everyone exuded joy without words.

The Dangly Tooth

William's class invested in his well-being. One day, I got a phone call from William's aide , "D." I lived close to the school and was home when I received her call. "Can I bring William home? He has a loose tooth dangling by a thread from his gums. I tried to pull it out myself, but he won't let me near him. He's really upset." D was the next person he trusted after me, so I told her to bring him home.

Once I removed the dangly tooth, and William was calm, I said, "you might as well leave him with me since school is almost over."

"Oh no," she warily replied. "You don't understand. The kids need to know he is okay." No one had ever seen William so upset before. "If I don't take him back, the kids won't be able to get back to work." The Pierce School had shut down. The students were too preoccupied with William's situation to concentrate on their ABC's.

From Integration to Segregation

I wanted William to be like other boys his age. I wished he could join a conversation without needing me to translate his out-of-context stories to people over and over again. I tried to accept that William was content to stare out the window and watch other kids play in ways he couldn't. I wanted him to read and write, drive, or have a girlfriend, and carry on his own conversations.

Halfway through first grade, it became apparent that academically, the Pierce School had outgrown William. In first grade, there were rows of desks, where it mattered if you wrote, walked, talked, read, and did the math. William wasn't a sit-at-your-desk-and-learn-the-three-R's type of guy. Teachers didn't have the experience to design the classroom for a student who would never learn to read, write, add, subtract, or walk the balance beam in P.E. William's friends were growing up. They were playing soccer and baseball, working out math problems, turning in science projects, reading their writing at the authors' teas, getting grades, riding their bikes, and jumping off the dock at the lake. William was not.

William didn't fit the Pierce School classroom, and the classroom didn't fit him. The leap between the first and second grade is a big one. Kids weren't listening to stories anymore. They were reading them. They were no longer playing with blocks. They were counting them. William wasn't learning to read, and he never would. He was having a hard enough time learning to talk.

I vacillated. If I kept William at the Pierce School, what would they do with him? Already, the staff was beginning to show signs of running out of the steam it took to invent things for William to do while the other students pursued academics.

I called the Disability Rights Center. I appreciated their die-hard approach to full integration for anyone with a disability. However, I knew the Pierce School did not have the resources to adapt their academic program to William's needs.

At this time, the school district had started a Life-Skills program, which was another name for a self-contained classroom where students would learn what they could. Life-Skills was at the other end of the swinging pendulum between William's total inclusion at Pierce to complete segregation ten miles from his community. The Life-Skills program would focus on his specific needs for speech, occupational therapy, and physical therapy. If William went there instead of Pierce, he would be with other students of varying abilities, outside of the mainstream of the school's population.

He would become Down syndrome William—one of the "SPED kids." Centralizing all people with significant special needs in one location was a matter of economy for the district. It slipped through the cracks of the movement to integrate all students.

As much as I grappled with sending William to Life-Skills or keeping him at Pierce, it was a matter of giving up or giving in. He was wasting time watching his peers learn at Pierce, and in his boredom, he was getting rambunctious. I started to doubt my conviction about full inclusion for William.

IDEA

The first attempt to secure equal access and equal opportunity inside schools originated with a law passed in 1975, the Education for All Handicapped Children Act. This legislation was revised and was renamed the Individuals with Disabilities Education Act (IDEA)."

"The Individuals with Disabilities Education Act ensures that students with a disability are provided with Free Appropriate Public Education tailored to their individual needs. This piece of American legislation has four-parts. Part A covers the general provisions of the law. Part B covers assistance for the education of all children with disabilities. Part C covers infants and toddlers with disabilities, including children from birth to age three. Part D consists of the national support programs administered at the federal level. (sites.ed.gov)

During William's tenure in the public school system, from birth to 21, the IDEA changed its wording four times. 1990, 1997, 2004, and after he graduated in 2015. In 2004, four years before William's graduation, "Congress reauthorized the IDEA. Then in 2015, they amended it through Public Law 114-95, the Every Student Succeeds Act, in December 2015." The law's most recent revision by Congress states:

> *"Disability is a natural part of the human experience and in no way diminishes the right of individuals to participate in or contribute to society. Improving educational results for children with disabilities is an essential element of our national policy of ensuring equality of opportunity, full participation, independent living, and economic self-sufficiency for individuals with disabilities."* (sites.ed.gov)

Currently, in 2019, William's district has moved closer to the literal interpretation of the law. Students with different abilities have moved into classrooms in the high school taking their Special education teachers along with them.

The IDEA leaves too much room for interpretation. Each of the three or four or five (I stopped counting in high school) Special education Directors who approved or disapproved William's Individual Education Plans (IEPs) and placements had different interpretations of the law. When William turned three, the Special education Director leaned toward inclusion. The second director, who took the job around the time I was grappling with whether or not to take him out of Pierce, supported segregating the students with her Life-Skills model. Both models were and are legal, depending on how the Special education Director interpreted the law. IDEA is loose enough to be interpreted in ways that can save the district money or in ways that serve the student.

The Path of Least Resistance

Some people followed the school district's path because it was the path of least resistance. Because I didn't know what else to do, I sent William to the Life-Skills classroom even though it meant leaving his people, his town, and his community. I made this decision with trepidation. Neither place was a good fit for my son. At least the decision would give me the chance to try the Life-Skills program while I thought of a better plan. For all I knew then, maybe it was a better setting for William.

The Life-Skills program didn't suit William. He survived it by doing things he didn't like to do. He did make some friends from distant towns, but mostly William was frustrated there. William's challenging behavior escalated. The team of teachers interpreted his frustration as inappropriate behavior despite the limitations of William's speech and his level of interest. They squashed William's soul and didn't take the time to understand who he was or what he was trying to say. I didn't like the way the teachers designed the program in the

Life-Skills room, either. It seemed to be designed to teach a student how to be disabled.

My choice to take William out of Pierce School was the biggest mistake I made in William's school career. Having to choose between two extremes of full inclusion or full segregation didn't leave me with much of a choice.

I couldn't fathom what it would take to mainstream him during his elementary school years short of tearing the school down and building a model school where, as the law said: "Disability is a natural part of the human experience and in no way diminishes the right of individuals to participate in or contribute to society." Integration was William's civil right. The Special education Department supported pooling all students with disabilities into one setting, as they believed this was the best approach to teach them how to participate in and contribute to society.

Even though it was my choice to put William into the Life-Skills program, I felt defeated. I had given up the fight to provide him a chance at a typical, heterogeneous life—the kind of life his sisters would endure through the bumps and lumps of public school. I was weary from my constant battle to fit William into a system that wanted to segregate him from the rest of our community. The injustice of this churning and festering inside me took its toll. I tried to hold it in, but it started to snowball. When I moved him into the Life-Skills room, he was right where the system wanted him to be.

All those years ago, I wondered where William would land when he became an adult. Would he ever have the sense of community Joan Schnare fostered at the Pierce School? Would there be another aide, like D, from the Pierce School to help him when things got tough? I carried the essence of his kindergarten year at the Pierce School with me as a foundation of what he could and should have throughout his life. Leaving the Pierce School meant giving this up for a while, but I could still pursue it as a model for his future education.

Three Wheeling

When William was a newborn, I formed a mental image of a man with Trisomy-21 riding his bike, and that image stuck with me. Around the time I put William into the Life-Skills Program, I bought him a tricycle. It was tailor-made, cost $2,500, and the Lions Club paid for it. It was hefty, sturdy, grounded, and metallic blue. It had a fixed-gear, so he controlled his speed by pedaling backward. It was a three-wheeler with a power he knew how to harness.

William had confidence in his three-wheeler that was hard for a mother to watch. He tore down the Summer Street hill in front of our house and hugged the ninety-degree turn at the bottom while the right rear wheel hovered above the pavement as he leaned into the curve. Once he rounded the bend, the trike righted itself, and he sailed along seamlessly. William sought sand patches for burning out on one of the rear wheels—an innate talent. He made motor sounds, sped forward to the next sand patch, again and again, lost in his world of boy-dom.

Riding up the Summer Street hill, was a battle of wills. As he approached the last leg, William's feet froze on the pedals. He ordered me to push him the rest of the way. I refused. He held his ground until something had to give. He was in lock-down mode.

I could feel neighbors watching or listening behind their curtains. William didn't care what they thought, but I did. The neighbors were imaginary witnesses to my life, judging my inadequacies as a mother raising a son she had no business raising. If I hadn't felt as if I was on center stage in the middle of Summer Street, I would have left him there to figure it out on his own. Instead, I faked it—every time. I put my index finger lightly on William's back until he broke away from me and motored up the hill with a surge of power.

William never became the man in the mental image I created on his third day of life; he never did ride his mountain bike into town. He can't ride his trike through the streets of Peterborough. He wouldn't know what to do if he fell, and there would be no one there to help him.

I watched the neighborhood kids ride their bikes over makeshift jumps they set up on the sidewalk. William didn't have the processing power to ride his bike the way they did or to make rapid transitions from bikes to basketball, skateboarding, or computer games. I was his biking buddy, his goalie for soccer, and his baseball compadre. I had to hold my breath when he hugged the corner. I had to let him be a boy.

Listen

Sometimes he sounds soft like a lamb.
I have to lean in
to turn down the marching band.
Say it again, William.

Sometimes, like Billy Goat Gruff—
anger with love mixed
underneath
the bridge—fearful emphasis echoing,
You
Don't
Know
Sometimes a question sounds like
HooUmm?
Like an owl cocking its head
curious eyes wide open

Sometimes a *no*
slides up the scale from
Billy Goat Gruff and crescendos to
owl tones at their height.

Grit

Upholding the title of an expert takes time and grit. I earned the expertise I acquired by making mistakes and learning how to make sound decisions about and for William. Grit was about believing in myself enough to know when I had chosen the right direction.

When you have a child with Trisomy-21, sometimes people assume you are an expert on the subject. The problem is you aren't. You never will be. I had some guidance, but I never had all the answers. I had to believe in myself enough to trust that I knew what was right for William. I had to make decisions about William for William. No one could make them for me. I was the one in charge, and I didn't always trust myself with this responsibility.

The bureaucratic system—Medicaid, Social Security Income (SSI), school, health, and state funding—was a tangled web of frustration. Unfortunately, this web of systems provides all of the things William cannot do without, including his housing, education, daily living expenses, and assistance for activities like skiing, Horse Power, taking trips to certain places, etc. The lack of common sense coming from these systems astounds me.

The state required William to take their standardized state tests even though he could not read, write, or hold a pencil, let alone understand any of the concepts. There was no getting out of that one. The state needed the statistics of all students, including William, so that they could tell the Special education department that they needed improvement.

I drew the line after taking William to a two-hour test to prove he had Trisomy-21—as if he no longer carried an extra chromosome anymore. Instead, I found a four-page test of ridiculous questions to defend his identity as a person who had Trisomy-21. I also had the results of the blood test he took as an infant if he failed the test.

I drew the line when his occupational therapist added a goal to William's Individual Education Plan (IEP) for William to cross the street, eighty percent of the time. I understood that each goal had to include a percentage. Still, when 20% of the target could result in a fatality, it was worth arguing the point. After many hours of standing my ground, the occupational therapist eliminated that goal.

I drew the line when his Sunday school teacher closed the classroom door before William could get there. I made our entrance dramatic enough to accentuate the teacher's insensitivity.

When the middle school principal called to say, "The fifth grade goes on a three-day trip at the beginning of each year. What do you want to do with William?" I was speechless. It was becoming a reality that William's new school supported segregation.

I drew many lines and tried to let go when I could, but this was and still is hard to do. I was fortunate to be an educator who understood the lingo of Special education. As a teacher, I have seen what happens to parents who don't have the means to figure things out the way I did. As a teacher, I witnessed the system's ineptitude in the field of Special education.

There are many ways to describe the journey someone makes when they raise a son or daughter with Trisomy-21. Some follow the path laid out for them by government mandates. Some, like me, mix and match to learn how to steer the course. Others may fight to integrate their children into the mainstream of the school system and society. Others may fall somewhere in the long line of options. I respect them for making the choices they do.

Ping-Pong

Trisomy-21 made me have to battle bureaucracy more than most parents. The educational and government systems don't see beyond William's Trisomy-21. A small handful of teachers did, but when it came to William's human side, the goal was always to make him as "normal" as possible. Normal meant not hugging when it was "inappropriate," moving faster than he could, reading, writing, being social, and communicating in a way he wasn't capable.

No one can keep up with the endless stream of things it takes to try and make someone normal. Doubt plagued me. William was not only my first child. He had Trisomy-21. All I knew was what I had stumbled upon along the way to get him to the fifth grade. Sometimes I thought, what if the school *is* right and I am wrong? Maybe I *should* segregate my child in case I am not right. It's like baptism. Even if you are not a believer, you might baptize your child just in case you are wrong in not doing so. It was a game of ping-pong, Am I right? Are they right? Am I wrong? Are they wrong? Right? Wrong? Who had the answer—the winning shot?

Guess What?

At home, my son wasn't William with Trisomy-21. He played and fought with his sisters, went on forays into the snowy woods in the red plastic sled I dragged behind me. He kicked off his boots when I pushed him on the swing for the pure joy of seeing where they would go. At the library, William pulled all of the books from his favorite reading shelf and dove into their magical picture worlds to the tune of his self-stimulating ayyaayayaayay. He listened to music, went grocery shopping with us, took swimming lessons, watched movies, went to Broadway shows, and rode his big trike.

I wanted him to be the same William outside of our home as he was inside it—independent, defiant, silly, and electric. I didn't want him to be "Down syndrome" William. I wanted him included like any other kid. The problem was he wasn't any other kid. At school, I wanted what he couldn't have. I wanted him to be in the band, to run around at recess. I wanted the other kids to be his mentors. Some people with Trisomy-21 can keep up and do all the things that I wanted William to do with his peers. William wasn't one of those people. He never learned to read, write, or do math. Transitions were and still are difficult for him, and he doesn't have the agility to keep up with his peers. For that to happen, I had to initiate and foster it. I took him on bike rides, on walks into town, to the library, and to places where he could interact with the world. At school, he had an aide or a teacher by his side. He didn't have the freedom to be himself without my help.

Trisomy-21 comes in many flavors. Some people with Trisomy-21 read, write, go to college, and give speeches. Others become actors, advocates, Special Olympic athletes, and artists. On the other end of the spectrum are people who cannot read, write, or do arithmetic. As a high school English Language Arts teacher, I can guarantee you that my "typical" students had a similar range. People who cannot read are not incapable of living rich and engaging lives. One of William's favorite pastimes is listening to storytellers—Odds Bodkins and Jay O'Callahan are his favorites.

Every once in a while, I will think, "I have a son who cannot read." And guess what? It doesn't matter.

Time

You need time to understand what he is trying to say.
Time to stroll.
Time to stop
and talk.
Time to spend hours in one spot doing the
same thing over and over again.
when everyone else races ahead.

Summer Break

Special education students have a program in the summer called the Extended Year Program (EYP) if the administrators think a student will regress. Every summer, the district would determine the likelihood of William regressing without summer school, and every summer, they decided that he would. The purpose of the Extended Year Program isn't for the student to progress. The objective is to maintain the status quo—as if a child ever stops learning and growing.

I know that children learn and grow as human beings without the restrictions of bells, standardized tests, and teachers telling them to quiet down and be still. What a student learns from days of swimming, riding bikes, traveling with family, and hanging out with friends is far more valuable than what they learn in the classroom. However, the idea of William regressing concerned me, so I erred on the side of the professionals and sent him to summer school. My self-doubt overruled my common sense.

Also, I needed a break. Those twenty hours a week of summer school gave me time to take my girls swimming, hiking, and adventuring without William's obstinacy about not doing those things. When William didn't want to go somewhere, he plopped on the floor, lifted his arms, tucked his loose shoulder blades into the low tone of his back. He was heavy and supple enough that there was nothing to hold onto to lift him from this position.

William preferred to stay at home, listen to his records, and play with his cars or Playmobiles. I was another person asking him to do what he didn't want to do. It wasn't fair for either one of us. There were times when bringing William along put us both into a funk. We lost all sense of spontaneity. I would get into such a lousy mood that nobody wanted to go anywhere with me anyway.

I sent William to summer school for my self-preservation. I had to find a balance between his needs, his sisters' needs, and mine.

Paper Footsteps

One summer day, William's physical therapist held a session at our house. She laid paper footsteps all over our lawn—not a piece of level ground for the quarter-acre we owned at the time. William and I looked at each other. We must have been thinking the same thing— *she wants him to walk over all of those footsteps?* At the end of the steps, the reward waited—hitting a T-Ball—which was something William loved to do, and he was good at it. She got the reward right, but getting the reward was not going to happen.

William knew it.

I knew it.

The therapist didn't.

William balked the minute he saw the footsteps. A behavior problem in the eyes of a Special education expert, a form of expression in mine. I didn't say a word. The therapist proceeded with her lesson, which consisted of William plopping down like a tired elephant. He used his shoulder move to make it impossible for his therapist to lift him to get him going. When his allotted half-hour of therapy ended, the therapist declared surrender, gathered her untouched footsteps, and went on to her next client. The physical therapist was kind-hearted and meant the best, but she was wasting her effort. I finally discontinued the physical therapy that the school system provided. I wasn't ready to give up on physical therapy altogether, so I found another therapist my insurance covered.

I called my insurance company first. They *did* cover William's physical and occupational therapy. Not only could I choose the best, and get the best, I didn't have to pay for it. However, if I hadn't called my insurance company first, I would not have found the therapists I did.

Finding Barbara

I knew Barbara would be William's physical therapist the minute I met her. Barbara was a problem solver, and she didn't need to
prove anything to anyone. She had a private practice, and she was her
own boss. She wanted to succeed, which meant William was going
to follow suit. Our goal was to get William to walk as smoothly and
comfortably as possible for him. William did anything she asked him
to—no floppy shoulder act for her.

I knew William would walk someday. The question was when.
In retrospect, I wonder why I was so pressed to get him to walk if
I knew deep down he would do so eventually. He still resorted to
scooching, and he moved around remarkably well. He didn't seem to
mind that he couldn't walk. I hoped maybe if he walked and talked,
his peers wouldn't leave him behind anymore.

Barbara wanted William to feel the fluidity of walking. I did not
know it at the time, but this is the purpose of therapeutic horseback
riding. The horse was a vehicle to expose William's muscle memory
what it felt like to walk. William refused to do many things, but riding
horses was not one of them. And Barbara had a horse.

Once, when I was picking up William after a session with Barbara, I couldn't find them. I went to the playground behind the building. At Barbara's suggestion, William wore orthotics, plastic braces that reached up his calves to give his low-toned legs more stability. I looked across the playground and saw Barbara holding William's hand, walking at a fast clip and pulling him along. William had no choice but to move with her, and he showed no remorse about doing it. When they completed their circuit, they had had quite a workout.

Barbara pushed William through the stopgaps in his gait so he could establish and feel his stride. She had spent the morning getting him to walk without giving him the time to think out every step. His trust in Barbara was the key to his progress, and William never knew what she had up her sleeve for another session.

Finding Barbara showed me I could find someone like her for occupational therapy.

Finding Staci

Staci had the same philosophy as Barbara—keep William moving instead of giving him the time to break down and process each movement he made. This approach helped William to feel the smoothness of motion. According to Staci and Barbara, William needed sensory integration, a process by which people receive information through their senses, organize this information, and use it to conduct everyday activities. When William's senses were overloaded, he flapped his hands, sucked on them, or made a self-stimulating sound to bring all of these senses together. Giving William sensory input in a structured and repetitive way would help him process and react to the sensory stimulation the world throws at us. He neither sucked nor flapped his hands in physical or occupational therapy because Staci or Barbara satiated his need for sensory integration in a measured dose.

When I arrived to pick up William after occupational therapy, I usually found him in a gym full of swings, scooters, rollers, and a giant play-pool full of plastic balls. William's reward at the end of the session was to immerse himself in a plastic pool full of tennis ball-sized plastic balls. Other times, I might find William folded over a swing on his stomach or propelling himself across the gym floor on a scooter. His reward was self-generated. The work and the effort he put into carrying it out was his reward.

Staci and Barbara proved how much more William was capable of when he was in the right hands. They showed me that pride is the best reward, and they gave that to William, who carried it around like a badge.

If the school cannot provide a service stated in the IEP, they are responsible for paying for it. Unfortunately, years later, my insurance company rescinded their support because they determined that Trisomy-21 was a pre-existing condition. When the district finally hired an occupational therapist, William had to go to the school for therapy even though it lacked the luster I had found privately. I did not bother reinstating his physical therapist.

Circle of Friends

Jim Orr was one of William's and my many guides throughout William's middle school years. Jim Orr's primary interest has always been in helping others who do not have the power to help themselves. He once went as far as breaking the law to protect someone he felt the system treated unjustly. I met Jim Orr when the school district hired him to transition Special education students from one school to the next. Eventually, they fired him because he fought for the cause of the students and not the school. He was our ally.

Jim Orr started a Circle of Friends meeting for William to gather people in the community already connected to William, who could support him. I rallied William's kindred spirits and people from our town of Antrim—his circle of friends—to visualize his future. Jim Orr brought in new people—police officers, firefighters, local business owners, and other community members.

When we gathered, Jim Orr encouraged me to examine what lay ahead for William. I passively pushed back with my anxiety about William's future. I struggled to look beyond the present because what if these hopes didn't turn into reality? Jim Orr opened the meeting with, "Imagine what you want for him in ten or fifteen years. What does he deserve to have?"

I turned on my okay-I-might-as-well-go-along attitude because I knew it took an open mind for me to come up with a plan for William's future. Having a circle of William's friends surrounding me made this easier.

The circle brainstormed and came up with a list of goals such as William will go to the local middle school and walk there on his own. He will march with and conduct the Temple Band. He will make his bed and get himself ready for his day. He will work with the local fire department, forge meaningful relationships, and have the support system to live independently.

My anxiety tried to protect me. I feared for his independence. I worried about his having to adapt to new routines. And what about loneliness, others taking advantage of him, other people's agendas, losing his network of support and friends, taking care of his mental and physical health, communication, sexual awareness, appropriateness, time, place, and his being able to get to places? Who would take care of him when Tom and I were gone? I feared what could go wrong instead of what could go right.

By the time Jim Orr finished the meeting, I had started to allow the future to seep in and pull me forward. People like Jim Orr kept me going at times when I felt like giving in to the system. Jim Orr's advice has always stuck with me: "You have to do what you think is best for William and prove you are right. Then the rest will fall into place." This lesson carried me far while I continued to face William's and my challenges. Sometimes I need to do what I know is right no matter how loud the chorus is of those who want him or me to follow. At this point, William had graduated from elementary school and was entering the middle school Life-Skills program.

Allies and Obstacles

While William was rising and falling, ebbing and flowing through his life, it felt as if someone was in the foreground, laying out giant plastic footsteps for us to follow. The local agency kept adults with disabilities engaged by sweeping the mini-mall parking lot. My expectation for William's future was so much higher than that. They might as well post signs on their backs, saying, "I am disabled."

When I mentioned this to his teacher, she retorted, "you have another thing coming." If she could say something like that to me, what was she teaching William?

The life-skills methodology taught the children in the program to stay within their limitations. In other words, William had to learn to do things their way despite his level of interest or ability. For example, his teachers and specialists used a reward system. William doesn't buy into rewards. Like for most people, the prize is in what you do. Otherwise, what is the point? One therapist rewarded him with a jig-saw puzzle if he finished his lesson! That reward was harder for him to complete than the original task.

The system pushed William to do what fell under the public school system's façade of normal. If I had let him grow and develop with the laissez-faire attitude I raised my daughters, he might have been better off.

Educators, Special education directors, cardiologists, neurologists, general practitioners, speech, physical, and occupational therapists, orthodontists and caseworkers, were just doing their jobs. But I was doing my job too. They didn't have time to understand what it was like to fight for my child the way I did. These people were supposed to be William's allies, not his obstacles. The obstacles in any journey teach us how to overcome them. When we reach our destination, we will have a deeper understanding of who we are when we get there.

The Least Restrictive Environment (LRE)

"An Individualized Education Plan (or IEP) is a plan or program developed to ensure that a child with an identified disability who attends public school receives specialized instruction and related services."

"To the maximum extent appropriate, children with disabilities…are educated with children who are not disabled, and special classes, separate schooling, or other removals of children with disabilities from the regular educational environment occurs only when the nature or severity of the disability of a child is such that education in regular classes with the use of supplementary aids and services cannot be achieved satisfactorily." (sites.ed.gov.)

The government mandates that anyone who has an IEP must have yearly goals and objectives in place each year. It is illegal to consider where the student will fulfill these goals before the parent signs off with agreement to the goals and objectives. The where is called "placement." Placement meetings come after the team writes the Individual Education Plan. This is because the IEP goals determine the least restrictive environment for the student. Therefore, the team can then decide where the LRE would be in accordance with the IEP. Only after the team determined William's needs, could they decide where they could meet those needs.

Although parents are supposed to be a part of the team, often they are pitted against the teachers, therapists, and educators. In the placement meetings I attended, it was usually me against seven or eight educators, therapists, and administrators. They knew that I wanted William to go back to his local school, so they stacked the team against me.

The illegality of not talking about placement before the team wrote the IEP was a win-win for the district and a lose-lose for William. I interpreted the least restrictive environment to mean what it says. The least means less—a place with the least. Restrictive means imposing restrictions or limitations on someone's activities or freedom. When I put those two terms together, freedom rings.

For years, when it was time to determine his placement, I wondered where William could be the least restricted. I never knew that by including occupational, speech, and physical therapy, I was eliminating any chance of his attending his local school. I would have dropped his therapies if it meant that he could go to school in his neighborhood. Instead, when I suggested goals for William, I had his freedom at the forefront of my calculations. I thought, if I write goals and objectives with his freedom in mind, then surely, they would let him back into the mainstream. That was my mistake. Since I couldn't grasp the district's interpretation of the phrase, I didn't know how to break the cycle. I was beginning to realize that my misunderstanding of the school's semantics was getting in my way.

For William's early middle school years, I continued to rely on my interpretation of least restrictive. Maybe I didn't want to believe that least restrictive applied to the district and not to William. In other words, the least restrictive environment was the place where the school could consolidate his therapeutic services. This saved the district time and money. The therapists didn't have to travel from school to school because the Special education students were all in the same place. Ironically, William's team, therefore, isolated him in the least restrictive environment by placing him in the only place the school district would provide services for him—the Life-Skills Room.

This environment was specific and measurable, as most things in Special education are. For the administration, it was the cheapest location they could place any special needs student while providing all of the services in his IEP at one site. Again, this was a matter of interpreting the IDEA in a way that favored the Special education department and not the student.

Out of the two middle schools in the eight-town district, one delivered the therapies specified in William's IEP. The least restrictive environment is not about the student at all. It's economical. The law is the law even though it can legally mean two different things, depending on how you look at it. The team decided if William continued with his speech and occupational therapy, he had to be bussed twenty minutes away from his community. This least restrictive environment mandate kept William from walking up Summer Street to his local school.

Get Your Foot in the Door

I knew the principal at the local middle school—at the top of the street where we lived. If anyone could help me get William into our neighborhood middle school, he could. He had turned his middle school into one of the best in the state. He had started as a special educator. How could I go wrong?

I met with him before William's placement meeting when the team would decide where the least restrictive environment for William would be. It is a strict rule that no one discusses placement until after the IEP meeting. I was beginning to understand why.

"I want William to walk to your school every day and be a part of his community. How can I make it happen?" I asked.

He said, "Figure out a way to get him in through the back door and leave the rest to me."

Epiphany

The team is anyone who works with William—his occupational, physical, and speech therapists, his Special education teacher, and the principal. I was supposed to be a part of the team, but I was an outsider, the one who rocked the boat. It was hard to be a member of a team when they wrote an IEP focusing more on the school's limitations than William's. In William's case, the Special education Director came to his meetings because she knew I disagreed with the district about William's placement. I made enough noise about what I wanted for William, so they brought everyone to the table they could muster. I brought Jim Orr. William's team was stacked in their favor—six of them to the two of us.

On the day of the placement meeting, I made one of the pivotal decisions of our lives. At the placement meeting, held in the largest room in the School Administrative building, I faced William's team. It was as if I was squaring off for a soccer game face to face with my opponent. Now, the team included the principal from William's local middle school. My pal, my partner in crime, was going to help me plead William's case for placement in the school two houses away from where we lived.

The principal from our local middle school opened the meeting, which always throws off the Special education Director because she is the one with the agenda. She is the one in control. I had used this tactic many times before. This was the principal I had talked to two days before the meeting. He wasn't God, but in my estimation, he was about to perform a miracle. He didn't have a flowing white beard. It was neat and cropped. He was a chiseled, articulate, intelligent man.

"Before we start the meeting," he said, "I want to be clear that our school would not be the least restrictive environment for William. We would in no way be able to support his needs there. We have no facilities to meet William's needs."

His betrayal came out of nowhere. Why did he bother to come? I wanted to believe he was sincere when I talked to him before. Maybe someone had gotten to him between the time we spoke and his declaration. My body drooped, and my mind went into overdrive. I learned at an early age, never to trust a soul, not even God. How could I have believed this principal who worked for this school district? Was it because I wanted what he could have given William so desperately?

There were nods of agreement, and murmured "of courses" and "absolutelies" swirling around the table. Obedient Adams and Eves, who never would have dared give into the snake's charm by seeing my side of things. Had I already taken a bite of the apple when I approached this man who had advised me—promised me—that all I had to do was get William's foot in the door and he would take care of the rest?

Words fell out of my mouth like icicles on a spring day. "I guess that ends this meeting then." Did I hear those icicles fall? "I am taking William out of your program." Once an icicle falls, it doesn't stop in midair or reverse direction. Still, it could shatter when it hits the snowbank underneath hardened by melting snow and freezing rain.

I don't know who was more shocked—them or me.

There was a vacancy in everyone's non-reaction. I had broken the law. An Adam and Eve law—one that challenged the placement law—when Eve challenges God and says, "Hey, why does one guy get all the knowledge? I should have some too." I took a bite of the apple from the tree of knowledge. In doing so, my inner-Eve had spoken.

Talking with the Department of Health and Human Services for the First Time

In the fateful placement meeting, I was rational enough to tell the school district that William deserved to continue with his speech and occupational therapy. Miraculously they complied. Maybe they knew they had pushed me too far.

When students follow the traditional special education path and comply with the public system, the Centers for Medicare and Medicaid Services (CMS) supplements the schools to provide all of the services they need. When I took William out of the public school system, they no longer had a legal obligation to cover any of those services outside of the school setting.

I had to learn about the bigger system lurking in the background to create a sustainable enterprise for William's education. I wondered what support the government would provide William.

The big umbrella to education, vocation, and eventually, adult living, is a bureaucratic maze. I knew I would have to face government bureaucracy when William became an adult. My immediate circumstance forced me onto the bandwagon earlier than most people, and I am glad that it did.

I called the Department of Health and Human Services (DHHS) to see if they could help finance William's program.

"Hello, Department of Health and Services, can you hold, please?"

Click.

Why do they ask? I thought. What if I said no?

"Hello?"

"Yes, I am Elizabeth Goodhue, William Cochran's mother, and…"

"Social Security number, please?"

"Mine? Or his?"

"His."

I dug his social security card out of my wallet. I had never used it before. "William is no longer in the public school system and…"

Before I could explain, "Okay. Can you hold, please?"

I listened to the 60s-rock n' roll musak stream over the phone, imagining a receptionist pushing buttons, putting people on hold, taking the next person in line, and returning to a flashing button. Minutes later, she picked up. "I am going to put you through to his case manager. Hold on."

Eventually, I got through. I explained who I was and the details about removing William from public school and asked the voice on the other end of the line if William could receive services from the DHHS if he was no longer in the public school system.

"I'm sorry," she replied. "I didn't hear you."

I repeated my story and question with patience I didn't know I had.

"I'm sorry," she repeated, "I am hard of hearing. Can you say that one more time?"

I felt like Garret Morris on Saturday Night Live popping over Jane Curtin's head and repeating in a yell everything she said. I raised my voice three decibels higher, retold the situation, and asked the question again.

"I'm sorry…"

I couldn't go on with this ludicrous situation. William's caseworker was hard of hearing. She was his caseworker. She still is.

"No," I raise the volume of my voice as loud as I could without being mean, "I am sorry. May I speak to your manager, please." She heard me that time.

"Hello?" A male voice answered the phone.

"First of all, can you hear me?"

"Yes, I can. How can I help you?"

"My son's case manager couldn't hear me. I just thought I'd check," I said, gritting my teeth to settle the rising bile in my stomach.

"Oh, yes," he replied, "she can't hear."

I decided to let that one go.

I repeated the story about William leaving the school district and asked what the CMS could do to help William. I found out he should have been receiving a stipend all along for small things I no longer remember. I knew that when he reached the age of 21, the CMS would provide him with funds for living and health expenses as long as he had no other income. The manager suggested that I see how much my insurance would cover for his physical and occupational therapy.

"Thank you for your help," I said.

I learned four things during that one-hour phone call:

Never explain anything to the receptionist. She doesn't want to hear it because she is too busy. Her job is to connect you to your person.

If your case manager can't hear, ask to speak to her manager.

Establish yourself as soon as you can with government agencies that support people with developmental disabilities to see what benefits your child should be getting. Then, when he or she does become 21, they will be familiar with you and you with them.

Remember your sense of humor.

Now What?

I had tipped the cart, and everything spilled into a mulchy mess. William's education had reached the absurd. He had joined the ranks of the SPED kids, part of a broken system that characterized children by IQ scores instead of their self-worth. When I pulled William out of public school in seventh grade, I didn't have a plan. I hadn't expected the meeting to turn the way it did. I hadn't expected those words to drop from my mouth, but I am glad they did. Now I had a chance to build the education program William deserved and from which he would prosper. Finally, I had heeded Jim Orr's advice—I had to take the first step, the first bite—and everything would fall into place.

Jim Orr volunteered to take William while I was at work until I could figure out an alternative. My brother gave me money to cover the cost of tuition at New Holland Vineyard School, and I paid a friend to assist William during the day. A friend of mine, who also has a son with special needs, was the director of the New Holland Vineyard School, which she built to meet her son's needs. The program worked for William socially, but his success stopped there. He was too obstinate about learning to be academic. My friend and I agreed that the school was not a good fit for William.

Another friend stepped up. Sandy, who had just completed her degree in Special education, picked up the baton and worked with William for the remainder of the year. She pulled together a schedule that worked for William. He had been working at Edmunds, the local hardware store, so she set up a payment system for William that he could understand. He learned the value of work by delivering and collecting their mail from the post office across the street. He learned to cross the street independently, 100% of the time. William experienced getting paid for what he did and the value of money. He also started working at the town market and skied once a week with Crotched Mountain Recreational Sports (CMARS). Staci and Barbara continued as his occupational and physical therapists. My brother John made all of this possible by offering to pay for this.

Jim and William

That fall, when Sandy took a job as an alternative program teacher at the Pierce School, her husband, Jim, took her place. Jim was a powerful man in character and physique. He had worked as the head of maintenance at the middle school I wanted William to attend for years. Between William and Jim, they knew almost everyone in town. Jim knew all of the teachers, janitors, secretaries, and most of the students at the middle school; everyone loved and respected him. William knew the rest of the town, firefighters, police, librarians, neighbors, local merchants, their customers; all of these people extended the same love and respect.

Taking William into the middle school at the top of our street, and finding a teacher who would welcome him into her classroom, wasn't a problem for Jim. Every day Jim took William to the Alternative Education Classroom, which was full of the "bad" boys who couldn't settle down and be "good." These ruffians melted like butter when it came to William. They took pride in knowing him. Their teacher attested that William's presence shifted the tone of her classroom. In the year and a half that William and Jim showed up, student suspensions decreased 100%.

William benefited socially, as well. He was and still is renowned for teasing people and not knowing when to stop. If he teased a friend, which meant William was doing something only he found hilarious, his friend wouldn't let him get away with it. Life may have given the students in the alternative classroom a more bitter pill to swallow than William, but they were not about to let William's antics go just because he had Trisomy-21.

He developed a close friendship with Patrick. Once, they were messing around on the way home, and William pretended to spit at Patrick, thinking it was funny. Patrick wouldn't speak to William for weeks. It was the first time life slapped William in the face. It hurt, but he discovered the boundaries to kidding around with Patrick this time. His new friends showed him there are limits to what a friend can or cannot accept.

The classroom teacher, Deb, pushed William as far as she could academically. Still, she knew what he needed, and she did not interfere with the social interactions that happened rightfully. She was another person who worked magic with William. She came across as tough as Joan Schnare did, and carried the same full heart. She taught William to accept the challenges life threw at him. William valued his friendships there and rekindled some friendships with previous classmates from the Pierce School. To this day, he carries a collection of those friends' school IDs.

During those two years, William moved at his own pace, in a world where people valued his work and enjoyed his company. He had a feeling of self-worth, faced new challenges, and could visit friends and neighbors with ease.

Dave who Lost his Leg

William's days with Jim went beyond the middle school classroom. William worked at Edmunds Hardware and Wayno's Market, rode his bike, skied, and visited people in Antrim where we lived before I divorced Tom.

William and Jim went to visit Dave, Jim's friend. Dave had lost his leg in a motorcycle accident. He looked comfortable in his wheelchair but was not as comfortable in his prosthetic. The first day they met, William and Jim found Dave in his wheelchair amidst mufflers, crankcases, fenders, front forks, and various other motorcycle parts scattered throughout the house.

"Hey, Dave," William asked, "Where's your leg?" William had never met Dave, and seeing his leg wasn't there seemed like an appropriate question for a curious teenager.

"I lost it," Dave said flatly. I am not sure if he added the details of how, or when, but the concept of losing a leg wasn't lost on William. Jim and Dave jabbered on about motorcycles and engines, while William rummaged about Dave's house, which looked more like a motorcycle repair shop.

It was time to go. William and Jim had jobs to do, people to see, perhaps a class to attend.

"Hey William, let's go," Jim threw his voice toward the back of the shop where William continued to rummage. "Watcha doin' buddy? Let's go!"

"Hol' on a second," William threw back.

"Come on, William," Jim tossed his voice like a tangled vine for William to rewind his way to the front room.

"Dave! Dave!" William emerged, holding Dave's prosthetic. "Dave. Dave. I found your leg."

Years later, I wrote this story about Dave in my writing group and read it to them because it's funny. A woman responded, "It is so good that you can make the best of bad things." I thought I had written a comedy. She heard a tragedy. I still need to remind myself that some people think having a son with Trisomy-21 is a misfortune. Although her comment ruffles the hair on the back of my neck, her statement isn't a reflection about William or me. It is a reflection of how she sees the world through a different lens than I do. I wanted to tell her all the funny stories about William I could so she could laugh about William and his encounters with the world.

The Devil and Daniel Webster

Once Jim Orr took William to see the mini-opera, *The Devil and Daniel Webster* to watch his father sing. They got there early enough to get a front-row seat. "Would it be better if you sat back there?" an usher suggested when he saw William.

"No, thank you," Jim said, "the front row is fine." They proceeded to the front row and sat in the center. William got into his theater position, sitting forward on the edge of his seat so it wouldn't flip back and squish him. The orchestra struck its first chord and captivated William. After the performance, the usher sought out William and Jim and apologized.

Often people question William's functionality directly. It is not always so easy to give a gentle response. Perhaps the best answer is, why don't you take him to the opera to find out?

The Toaster Oven

William always wants me to tell the toaster oven story. He doesn't have the words to say to me why he did what he did. On the rare occasion when I turn on the stove or oven, he turns it off, knowing I will burn something, which is often the case. I am a danger in the kitchen. Therefore, I must have instilled something in William to raise his curiosity about fire and the process of heating things. Perhaps, he had seen me burn so many things, set off so many smoke detectors, leave burner marks on cutting boards, or stamp out potholders, that he had to experience the process first hand. I have started and put out chimney fires and melded teapots to the coils of the stove, causing electricity to arc through the kitchen. Smoky houses are no cause for me to panic. I have experience in that field.

William is Mr. Safety. The first thing he checks out when entering a house is the smoke detector. He is not the kind of person who would run out the door and down the street, burn himself on the stove, or stick scissors into a light socket. He is tentative about things like that. Also, he used to make a self-stimulating sound when he was engaged in something, so I could always hear where he was.

The toaster oven event took me by surprise. I was upstairs gathering debris for the wash or reading to Kate when I smelled smoke. It was a warm day for March, so I knew I had not lit the woodstove. Smoke curled its way upstairs. The smoke detector battery could have died ages ago. I checked the dining room wood stove at the base of the stairs—cold steel. I strode through the kitchen to check the living room stove with the same result.

I returned to the kitchen to find flames licking the wall behind the toaster oven. With the power and instinct of Wonder Woman, I grabbed the flaming toaster oven, rounded the corner to the mudroom, opened the door, and threw it into a snowbank.

There was evidence of two plastic spice containers melted into the rack of the toaster oven after I retrieved it from the snowbank. Their tops still stacked on the counter by the blackened wall where the toaster oven once sat. There was a little boy who watched me with a marvelous smile.

There is no mystery to this story. William and I don't discuss consequences such as these because he does not have the words to describe abstract thoughts about why he does what he does and when. Besides, I was there with him. I know what happened.

There was nothing to explain.

It happened.

He did it.

And we are left with a story to tell.

Speaking Cochranese

Once in middle school, William and Kate were in a class together. He was trying to be understood, so she translated for him. Jim said to her, "Oh yeah, I forgot you speak Cochranese." He was referring to their last name, Cochran.

William's language is purposeful yet difficult to understand, but his family gets the gist of what he is trying to say. However, sometimes even we cannot understand him either. Everyone should know what they miss by not learning "Cochranese."

One day as we were driving somewhere, William started a conversation.

"Mom, c' mere."

"What William?" I responded, thinking, *I am here*, but to him, I am not there unless I am looking right at him.

"Mom."

"Will, I am listening. I cannot take my eyes off the road. Go ahead."

"Talkies for Rich?"

"You're going to use them with Mr. Solito?"

"No. Not."

"Are you talking about the Walkie-talkies?"

"Yeah."

"What? Are you going to take them to Edmunds with you and Rich?"

"No, No, No."

"When are you going to use them?"

"Rich …"

"Does Rich have a set of Walkie Talkies?"

"No, a radio."

"You want a radio to go along with the Walkie Talkies?"

"Yeah."

"Does Rich have a radio?"

"No."

"But you need one?"

"Ya."

"So, you can radio to him when you go to work?"

"No."

"Are you going to show him your Walkie Talkies today?"

"Mom," he said, signaling the end of the conversation, "N'er mind."

The Wonderful
World of William

    William can throw a line from any of his favorite show tunes or Disney films. In the days of VHS, he watched them forward *and* backward. I limited his watching because he started to turn into a Buzz Lightyear-Professor Hill combination. William loves everything Broadway, *The Phantom of the Opera, South Pacific, Camelot, The Music Man, Oklahoma, Singing in the Rain,* the list goes on forever. Dick Van Dyke is Burt Dyke. Although he always asks me if Julie Andrews is good, we both know she is.

    William talks about his vast repertoire of films, which also include *The Wizard of Oz, Mary Poppins, Star Wars, Beauty and the Beast, Shrek,* and *Toy Story*. Sometimes it is hard to sort out which film or song he is referring to when he segues into a movie because of something someone says or does to remind him of it. If you are bald, you will remind him of Yul Brenner in the *King and I*. If you are black, he compares you to Eddie Murphy in *Shrek*. If you wear a cowboy hat, you are Tom Hanks or Woody from *Toy Story*. These are high accolades coming from William. When he makes those connections,

I don't want to be his translator, but he persists, and I try to brush it off. Sometimes his perseverance wins, and I am precise in my translation. So far, he has gotten away with it.

He knows about the actors and the films they have been in, who they played, and whether they are living or dead. He also does a passable imitation of all of them. His attention to detail takes people by surprise. In the *Wizard of Oz*, William knows which characters become the scarecrow, the lion, the Tin Man, the Wizard, and the Wicked Witch when the world turns from black and white to color.

Once during a cardiology check-up, William said, "I am the Tin Man."

"The Tin Man?" Dr. Flanagan questioned.

"Ya. I haven't got a heart."

Another time, when the community theater presented the musical *Oklahoma*, William crushed the opening scene when Curly made his grand entrance: "No horse?" he belted out a little too loudly. I had to agree. Who sings "Oh What a Beautiful Morning" when he isn't riding a horse? Maybe that was why Curly was out of tune.

Arguing with William

William and I argue about the realities of many films.

"What happened to Chitty Chitty Bang Bang?" William asks me frequently.

"It burned and was sent to the junkyard," I reply.

"No. Not."

"William, it did. In the beginning, it catches on fire. When Burt Dike gets the car, it's all black and burned," I repeat knowingly.

"Nope." Then through an explicit array of sound effects, his tiny hands arch out to show Chitty Chitty Bang Bang veering off to the side of the road in the introduction to the film. Somewhere in there, he reminds me that Chitty was avoiding a dog on the race track, and then the sound of a crash. He has a point. I missed that detail even though we have watched the film more times than I can count. But the car does catch fire eventually.

"William, why do you ask if you already know?" I don't like losing an argument.

He smiles, knowing he is right.

Occasionally, William still uses sign language to give me hints about what he is trying to say. Sometimes he makes up signs to clarify things. One day, William kept tapping his left shoulder with his right hand. We had watched Mary Poppins recently, but I needed more.

"William, you have to say something else or give me another sign."

He tapped his shoulder and said in his rendition, "Votes for Women." After the umpteenth time, I understood. It just took me a while to fit the pieces of the puzzle together. If you remember Mary Poppins, Mrs. Banks sings a song proclaiming votes for women. She marches about raising her arm across her banner to her shoulder. It's my favorite part of the movie.

Reception

William's speech is difficult to comprehend because he has a small mouth, low muscle tone, and difficulty with sensory processing and tactile feedback. One misconception is that William doesn't understand what people say to him because he cannot talk well, which is far from the truth. William understands the subtleties of language—its tones, rhythm, people's expressions, and emotions.

Most of the time, people can't understand what William is saying. Some people nod quickly, say yes, or avert their eyes, feeling shy about asking him to repeat himself. Others ask me for a translation. I wonder if people think William doesn't make sense—that what he says doesn't mean anything.

William's language can be a challenge because his context is all-time. It is often like Charades. Sometimes I inquire about the setting or background to get a more explicit hint of what he is trying to say.

"Are you talking about a movie?"

"No, not."

"A person?"

"Nope"

"What you did today?"

"Ne' r mind."

Or if I say, "William works with Rich," William will deny it. If he didn't work with Rich on that day, then it does not apply. Even if I can understand his words, his logic challenges me. I continue to try and understand everything he says without having to translate it in my head a million times. There are times when I wish William could join a conversation instead of asking me to retell his out of context stories to people over and over again.

Barbies and Kens

When I read about people with Trisomy-21, I often read about ballet dancers, Little Miss Americas, Little League Wonders—the plastic Barbies and Kens of the Trisomy-21 world. These are stories about adults who live independently, go to college, get married, drive, and star on TV shows.

Does anyone write about ordinary people with Trisomy-21? The average guy who hates to hike, but loves to downhill ski, listens to show tunes and military bands, but hates it when you sing along, who loves being on stage, but refuses to dance, who rides a giant tricycle so he can spin out the back tire, who doesn't read or write, and who speaks a different language only family and close friends understand?

The Barbies and Kens of the Trisomy-21 world can do what other people can do. The positive publicity is educational. However, not everyone has to or can be a superstar. Some of us who never make it to the top are still great.

I used to watch the neighborhood kids skateboarding on the corner and wonder what it would be like if William could do that.

What would it be like to say as he ran out the door with his skateboard, "Don't forget your helmet, William! Are you wearing your knee pads?"

My stomach had stopped churning when my friends' children passed William in the milestones the rest of the world takes for granted—walking, talking, losing teeth, learning to read, scoring home runs, becoming a student of the month, the angst of middle school, getting braces, having a gaggle of friends, talking about teachers, and participating in school assemblies and contests. Eventually, William did some of those things. And when he did, it was colossal.

Walking on

I had to leave for work earlier than my children left for school, so I left William and the girls with a sitter. It was time to test the old IEP goal I used to laugh at, which said: "William will cross the street 80% of the time." This time it had to be 100%. In increments, William gained the confidence to walk to Jim's house by himself.

After school, he walked to the Bryer's house, next to the school, where he stayed until I got home. William loved it there so much; he frequented their house to grab a bagel and watch a movie. Todd Bryer also took him to check the fire department's equipment every Sunday. When Tom or I went into a store in town with William, William stood outside and watched the cars go by until he got bored and walked home. Concerned neighbors or community members called me when they first saw him walking home alone from Edmunds or the Antrim Market until it became commonplace.

The community had his back. Pulling William out of the system and creating one that worked, turned out to be the best decision I could have made for him. I learned what I wanted for him and determined what I wanted his education to look like. People can survive without learning to read or write. I held onto the chance that he might learn, but enough was enough, now he needed to explore the real world and interact with it. Worthy people supported him, and they made it possible to create the best program for him. All I had to do was follow Jim Orr's advice to take the risk first and present the outcome when it worked.

William's new plan worked, but it was a personal and financial challenge to sustain it. My brother supported it financially, which made more difference in my life than he will ever know. But I couldn't rely on that forever, and besides, the school should have been paying for it.

Returning to School
on My Terms

One night during my insomnia worries, I realized the public school system could charge me with truancy. Any time, the truancy officer could come banging on my door to haul William back to the Life-Skills program. They didn't know that William was attending a different kind of school.

I went back to the Special education Director two and a half years after I had removed William from the public school system when William was in eighth grade. We gathered in a small room. This time the ratio was four on my side to two on theirs. I was as calm as a star settling into oncoming daylight. Jim Orr had been right, once I had a clear vision of what I wanted for William and followed it, then when I asked for it, I would have evidence to back up its implementation.

In the last meeting I had with the Special education director and her team, I hadn't known what lay ahead for William. My impulsive decision to take him out of school daunted me then. However, at this meeting, I wasn't giving up. It was time for the school district to pay for William's education. I had nothing to lose, and my previous actions resulting in taking him out of the school system had boosted confidence.

Now, I knew what I wanted for William. I knew the path I could forge for him was better than anything the Special education Director could muster. I had the power of ethics, creativity, love, and my son's years of experience outside of the system. The Special education Director had the power of clout, bureaucracy, and the law. I wore soft, fragile ornaments to her armor, but I had mastered the riddle, learned the game.

When you want something enough, you have to take a risk to get it—leap tall buildings in a single bound, have more power than a locomotive—but you can be subtle about it. Superman was a show-off with his uniform and his slick hair. He had special abilities, but he also had a habit of swooping in and then disappearing to become someone he wasn't. He didn't need to do that, and neither did I. This time, I took a leap with the determination I needed to steer William's course in one single moment.

Pulling Through

Before I had set up this meeting, I had called Monadnock Developmental Services (MDS) one of the local providers for people with special needs. MDS steers the State's ship through the waters of the sea of bureaucracy. MDS has been one of my many guides through the maze of systems supporting William. It is one of the numerous state-supported organizations providing people with intellectual and physical challenges with support. MDS funnels William's money from the state and the federal government into the big picture of William's life from early intervention for ages zero to three, the school from three to 21, and finally adult life.

They knew William and me well because I had leaned on them when I took William out of school. Commonly, people use MDS to get help for adult life when they get dumped on the boundary of the school district and adulthood. Leaving the traditional school system was an extra transition, and I needed someone to guide us through it. I needed someone who held as much clout as the Special education Director did—another bureaucrat from a different branch of the system.

Not only did MDS agree to come to the meeting, but a woman named Kerry shadowed William's day with Jim to see what William did. At the end of the day, Kerry couldn't stop raving about it. She thought what William and Jim were doing was cutting edge. It was bona fide inclusion that met the needs of William's Individual Education Plan. By engaging in work, he felt needed and valued. In a school setting, William's peers modeled social behavior for people his age. My program bolstered William's independence and confidence and brought him back to the community and those who knew him well, from students to neighbors, to the woman who saw him walking home by himself at the end of the day. After Kerry's observation of William's day, she agreed to come to the meeting to defend William's program, and she would bring her husband Chris, who was the Director of Adult Services.

Bamboozled

Chris started the meeting by telling the Special education Director that the district should support William's program. William's Life-Skills teacher stammered, "I'm feeling a bit bamboozled here. I thought we agreed the Life-Skills program is the least restrictive environment for William."

I had a hard time not bursting with laughter when I heard her say this. The only person I have ever heard use that word was W.C Fields. "Don't let them bamboozle you...but I never drink anything stronger than gin before breakfast." William's ex-teacher was no longer a threat to Will's program. She was teetering on the edge of ridiculousness.

"Have you observed William's day?" Kerry retorted.

Now the teacher had a reason to feel bamboozled. "Well, no," she mumbled.

Kerry was aghast that this teacher could be so obtuse and unprepared. "Do you know he spends part of his day in his local middle school? That he works three jobs? That he walks to school on his own?" Her disgust with the ignorance on the other side of the table dripped off each word.

William's ex-teacher crumpled in her chair and deferred to the Special education Director, who put in her final pitch, "William belongs in the Life-Skills program, which is, by law, the least restrictive environment for him." She didn't sound as forceful as she had in the meeting before.

There wasn't anything else to say. I was right about the course William was taking. They were wrong. But we had reached a standstill.

Chris stepped in to end the meeting. As everyone rose to leave, he suggested, "Why don't you wait outside? I'll talk with the Special ed. Director, to see if we can come to an agreement that works for William."

I walked out discouraged, but not surprised by the Special education Director's rejection. When Kerry had asked if the opposition had observed William's current program, I had some hope we might have won this unremitting battle. Now I wasn't so sure. It was a short wait. When the Special education Director made her exit, Chris said, "We're all set."

"What did you say to her?" I asked incredulously.

"I told her you had a strong case against the district. Then, I told her that if you wanted to send William anywhere else, you would win in court." He smiled and asked, "Do you know there are places close by where William could be educated at the cost of $150,000 a year?" It would be expensive for the district to go to court with us, and even more costly if I won. I would never have sent him to a campus that was only for people with disabilities and brain injuries anyway. I never considered fighting a court battle with the school district.

An hour after I got home, the Special education Director called, "We would like to try the program you have set up for William."

The next year, William and I had another transition to face. It was time for high school. This time it wasn't so hard. I worked in the same high school, and I had seen the respectful and gentle demeanor of his new teacher. William went into the high school Life-Skills program, keeping the same routine we had established for him before, with new people to help him through his day. The district provided occupational and speech therapy that was practical and applicable to his life. Now William was with all of his friends from around the district.

Fiddler

When auditions at William's high school for *Fiddler on the Roof* came up, I knew he had to be in it. However, being in *Fiddler* meant finding someone willing to help William participate. Otherwise, he would get lost in the logistics of what it would take to act in a play, If someone wasn't there to guide his way, maybe he wouldn't know what to do, or people wouldn't know what to do with him. For William to participate, he would need support. Since there were six weeks of rehearsals, at least three hours every weeknight, and on Saturdays, he needed more than a volunteer could provide. I thought of using respite money—money supplied by the state to give caretakers support—to pay someone, but there wasn't enough. The cost for endless hours of rehearsals and production would have been exorbitant.

Could I have dropped him off at the front curb of the high school and let him join the rehearsals by himself? Would he have taken his place with all of the other Yiddish actors on stage? What would he have done during the endless hours of green room time? Would someone have stepped up and guided him along? Would he have waited for me at the school's entrance without ever going to the rehearsal? Maybe if I dropped him off, he would have plunked down in one of the theater seats and just watched. But I wanted him to be in the show. I wanted him to experience the other side of the action, rather than being a member of the audience.

So, I volunteered to do the job. Not only did I have to switch hats and hang out with my students in the green room, but I also had to be a Russian peasant in Tevye's village. I don't dress up for life, and dressing up as a Russian peasant threw me far from my comfort zone. Still, I tried to be inconspicuous support for William.

William and I missed the choreography rehearsal for one of the biggest song and dance numbers in the show. In this scene, Tevye—the father and protagonist—fabricates a nightmare to convince his wife to break tradition and let their daughter marry for love. The dance reenacts his dream with the chorus sweeping back and forth, exhaling Yiddish exclamations of fear and terror to the ghost of Tevye's mother-in-law. I held William's hand and wiggled our way into the dance, which would have been a challenge even if we had learned the choreography. The chorus jostled around me because I had not been choreographed into the scene.

At first, I tried to pull William into the fray with me, but he stood his ground. He had the wherewithal to hang back rather than make a complete fool of himself like me. I tried to blend in while William tugged me in the direction I wanted to take—the sidelines. The chorus lugged me to and fro, like sailors hauling an anchor, away from William toward the ghost of Tevye's mother-in-law screeching like a banshee as we sang,

A blessing on your house
Mazel Tov, Mazel Tov

Forward and back, jostle and hustle, I went until the dance ended, and the cast made an exit into the dark wings of the tiny theater.

William was better off being a Russian peasant without me. He didn't mind his peasant costume, and being on stage was the best seat in the house. I put William in the bar scene with other raucous teenaged men dancing the bottle dance, clanking steins, and singing *l'Chaim, l'Chaim to life* at the top of their lungs. It was a scene for men. I was glad not to be a part of it, and William was a natural without me galumphing about at his side.

Today, when we talk about *Fiddler*, William doesn't reminisce about the nightmare dance, the l'Chaim scene, or the green room talks. "Mom," he says, "Sam played Tevye. Who died? Was he good? Who played the fiddler? Who danced the dance?"

What did William have to say?

Someone asked me,
does he talk about your part in the play?
William doesn't talk about things like that.
He talks about things I've done that made him laugh.
Like getting the car stuck in the mud,
the dog jumping out the car window,
falling down, burning food.
He doesn't tell me about his day.
He doesn't talk about what he does when I am gone.
He tells me about music, shows, videos—
endless streaming—
reruns of his past.

Turning Eighteen

When William turned eighteen, I decided to celebrate his life in a BIG way. I wrote a birthday party list of all of the people who had touched his life. The list went back to the one nurse who acknowledged what I was going through the day William was born; to Dr. Jean, the pediatrician who helped us find someone to make him well; to Dr. Flanagan, the cardiologist who saved him; to Swift, who showed up like magic, seconds after William went into his heart surgery. I invited the people we met in Children's Hospital, his first-grade teacher, Joan Schnare, his aide, D, the town police, firefighters, the friends he made in elementary, middle, and high school, his neighbors, and extended family. The list amounted to 150 people, and most of them came.

One of these people was Ross. He and William had been genuine best friends when they were in kindergarten, first, and second grade. Ross and William understood mischievous boy humor. I do not know who taught whom the mastery of it, but they made each other laugh, and at the same time, they made others laugh.

At the time of William's eighteenth birthday, Ross was the star pitcher of the high school baseball team. He was good-looking, popular, and in our small New Hampshire community, he was a baseball hero. When Ross came to William's party, I could feel the connection he had with William even then. Ross came alone, which spoke for him. William was a part of him and vice versa. Ross was a star, and he came back nine years later to reunite with his friend.

Do I Know?

People from high school remember you.
The king of I-want-to-know-him
across the board of the good, the bad, and the ugly.

If you knew then what you know now
would you live your life the same way?
or is now a continued then?

Would you say your best friend in the world was Ross
back then?
or are your best friends
remembered in the present tense?

Did you know
it took more effort for you to get through
the day than your classmates?
Would you say,
"I tried so hard?"

I used to think you had a secret sense
that told you everyone was good
even Gaston, Ursula, Cruella DeVille, and Buzz Lightyear's father.

I have always been your voice—
your translator,
but do I know what you know?

Another Happy Birthday

When one of my colleagues found out she was carrying a child with Trisomy-21, I was so psyched. Soon I would have someone I could help guide through this time so that when her son entered the world, it would be a time of celebration. Since she knew during pregnancy that her son had Trisomy-21, she could celebrate his birth rather than going through the adjustment period that I had.

During a faculty meeting, when my colleague was away, another colleague announced that Kristen was going to have a baby with Down syndrome. He suggested we give her support during this challenging time. Shoulders sank, and murmurs of "poor Kristin" circled the room. People suggested sending her flowers. "Maybe we should pretend we don't know, " someone suggested, "This is a private and personal issue."

"Let's send her a card to cheer her up," someone else chimed.

As the faculty brainstormed about how to make something so awful better, I wished someone had had the same conversation about me, but I didn't know William had Trisomy-21 until after his birth. After William was born, sympathy cards from my parents' friends, and some from my own friends, flooded my mailbox. They were so sorry.

"What a disappointment this must be," some wrote.

"I am thinking of you during this hard time."

One day as my mother rocked William, I looked up from a pile of sympathy cards and said, "I can't read these anymore." I was sad. I already loved William, my son, who was a part of me, the purest form of love, so soft and warm.

If the discussion had continued as it was, Kristen was in for the same experience I had had eighteen years ago. I regret that William's first day was not a time of joy and celebration. Luckily, I was there to tell her colleagues that this was not a time of mourning.

When I later told a friend about this event, her reaction was, "Did they even know you were in the room?" I had never thought of that.

I was so used to the insensitivity around having a child with Trisomy-21 that I didn't notice how callous this was. I was so used to students, colleagues, friends, and relatives saying, "that is soooo retarded," that I didn't acknowledge that the faculty, my colleagues, who knew William, were having this discussion. But this was about Kristen. This was about setting it straight for the people who had no idea that this was not a time for mourning.

I faced the faculty for my colleague, "This is a time of celebration. Kristin is having a baby. Let's send her birthday cards and celebrate this birth."

Allies

That year a woman at the community center started a group of students who called themselves ALLIES—an acronym that is long gone from my memory. This group made high school inclusive. William was not and never has been a scholar. Many die-hard inclusionists advocate for full inclusion in academic settings. I am glad that they do. However, an inclusive classroom never worked. I wasn't going to put him into a class just to prove that it was his right to be there.

ALLIES originated from the community center in Peterborough. The organization wanted to promote social inclusion for adults. What better place to do it than in the social mecca for teenagers—the local high school. A skeptic could see this as another fabricated and awkward way to integrate people with disabilities into a group of typical peers. You might envision van loads of people getting dropped off at Walmart to shop, or McDonald's to eat. ALLIES was quite the opposite. It attracted students from all of the school's social striations—people who felt they did not belong and those who did: jocks, geeks, the popular and the not so popular, and everyone in between. People in the mainstream needed a group like this as much as William did. This made ALLIES a unique group with gravitational pull.

The premise of the group was much like unified sports, except it was social. Once the group jelled, people went out to the movies or hung out at each other's houses. Sometimes they went on group picnics, or to a basketball game together. Sometimes they played a game of pick-up basketball—friendships formed between individuals who wanted to do something with one person. ALLIES made high school a social and positive experience for William and for people who wanted to feel a sense of belonging. People became genuine friends who looked forward to being with William without the reward of pay, but with the bond of friendship.

ALLIES changed the culture of high school. Teachers and students brought William into the fold. William acted in five plays, conducted a choral performance, continued to ski, went to the movies and parties, swam, went on bike rides, kayaked, rode his trike in a triathlon, canoed, and camped. He was popular.

During William's senior year, ALLIES had a prom on the same night as the high school had one. The prom can put pressure on people to look beautiful, to have a partner, to outshine everyone, and be popular. As someone who never went to the prom, I know I would have chosen to go to the ALLIES prom, which welcomed anyone no matter what they wore, or whether or not they had a date. There was no king and queen. People wore what made them feel beautiful—some wore shorts with a coat and tie, others jeans and tee shirts, and some went all out with gowns and ruffles.

William wore a bow tie, a button-down shirt, and his grandfather's tuxedo jacket. His date, Emily, was radiant in her dress, sandals, and perfect hair. William, knowing what made her feel grounded and safe, made sure she was in a comfortable space. Emily reciprocated. Their prom picture shows them, two of the most beautiful people I know, loving each other, trusting each other, and emanating joy.

When everyone in the group graduated, ALLIES graduated too. ALLIES devolved when members went to college, traveled, or joined the workforce. Years later, it morphed into CMARS, Crotched Mountain Accessible Recreation and Sports. William skies with CMARS every year with this diverse group of individuals.

William and Em

People ask me if William is capable of having a girlfriend, and I wonder if I have not exposed the people I know and love to William enough for them to know the answer. Can people exist without love, loving, and being loved? That is a rhetorical question. Anyway, there is no doubt about it. William loves Emily. Emily loves Will. But Emily loves a lot of people.

William knows Emily's discomfort with large crowds, loud noises, and little children. "Relax William," Em says when he flaps his hands. They hug, hold hands, and sneak in as many kisses as they can, but they haven't gone beyond that. Neither Emily nor William spend their time together alone.

I am not opposed to William having a consensual sexual relationship. However, Emily's parents know their daughter Emily isn't capable of making a judgment call as big as this one. I respect that. William does too, maybe because I have told him so, or perhaps because we don't leave them to their own devices.

If William has a relationship with a partner, and they show signs of sexual affection, I would be responsible for assuring William had birth control. The American School of reproduction says, "Although

166

Trisomy-21 males have been reported to be infertile, it may not always be true. Infertility in males has been attributed to defective spermatogenesis." If the situation arose, would I be responsible for him getting a vasectomy. It seems obvious that a vasectomy would be the best solution, but even when he had surgery on his heart, I struggled to make decisions about what doctors do to his body. As his guardian, I have the legal right to make this decision for him, but do I have the moral right? I don't think so. What right do I have to make decisions about his sexuality when he cannot express how he feels about it?

Forgetting

Raising William is not so different than raising any other child. You love, laugh and play, go on vacations, to school events, and everything else a parent signs up for when they choose to have children. But there is always something extra—avoiding stairs and escalators, trying to understand him, tying his shoelaces until you find shoelaces that don't need tying, zipping his jacket, administering medicine, and holding his hand—forever.

Once, I told my friend Karen how intense it must be for our mutual friend Mary to raise Raf who has challenges and does not have a diagnosis. "What an incredible woman Mary is," I marveled, "to face the challenges the way she does. Raf never stops, and she works so hard to make sure he is in a place that fits him and not the other way around. She even started The Field School for Raf where everyone had an IEP no matter what his or her ability was." I ended my prattling about Mary being one of the most dedicated advocates for her child I knew. I added, "Don't get me started on Cindy and Kathy, who are also amazing."

When I told Karen I couldn't imagine what it was like to be in Mary's shoes, she seemed puzzled. Here I was, William's mother, spouting praises about someone who, in Karen's eyes, was doing what I was doing, maybe more, and certainly not less. Here I was saying what other people said about mothers of children with different abilities.

I forgot.

Pride

Sometimes William's Trisomy-21 label fades. I don't feel like a heroine for doing what I do. I am an average mom. People often insinuate that parenting William makes me a superstar. I don't see it that way. I was raised to be humble. Growing up, my parents expected me to be stalwart and better than everyone else, but never to boast about it.

I read a piece from this book in my writing group, and afterward, someone asked me if I was proud. "Proud? Proud of what? That I wrote the story?" I had no idea what he was talking about.

"Proud of raising your son," he replied.

"No," I was at a loss of what to say.

Later, he told me that I needed to take out parts of my book that were self-deprecating, and I still didn't understand. I didn't recognize that by saying I was an average mom, I was not giving myself the credit I deserved.

When he said, "You are my hero in this book. I don't want people insulting my hero," it made sense to me. I never thought about my pride. I never held the same pride for myself that my readers or others might. Maybe I should be proud.

Functionality

Dictionary.com defines functionality as "the quality of being suited to serve a purpose well; practicality."

Someone once told me I was beating up my readers, who may have asked me about William's functionality. Some people who read this book might say, "I asked her that!"

I don't want to scold people for asking something that they didn't know was wrong. I do want people to think about how the question would sound to them if the same thing were asked of their child. This won't always work because some parents can't stop putting their kids on a pedestal no matter how they function. People who have kids with Trisomy-21 are guilty of that too.

My upbringing taught me never to brag. I was supposed to be a champion by being one, while at the same time not talking about it. In elementary school, I was a failure. I spent my fair share of time dragging my desk into the hallway as a punishment for not understanding, getting frustrated, and acting like the other bad boys in the class. I got Fs on my report cards from kindergarten to sixth grade. So, I had to prove my worth by being popular and athletic. Which luckily, I could do. But I confused pride and bragging. To this day, it makes me cringe when someone puts him or herself on a pedestal. Because when someone puts him or herself on a pedestal, everyone else belongs on the rungs below you.

Is that why the functionality question socks me in the stomach every time someone asks about it? Is it because I don't allow myself to brag about William? Is it because his tenacity, affection, humor, and empathy don't count in the high functioning department? Or is it because society puts so much pressure on people to prove their greatness. I don't know how to answer questions that hurt. I don't know how to answer the question of functionality without making William sound like he is less than he is. It makes me defensive because, by academic and social standards, he is not high functioning. Would high functioning mean I am one of the lucky ones? Should low functioning dash one's hopes?

The definition of functionality—"the quality of being suited to serve a purpose well"— doesn't call for negativity. Why is it so difficult to respond to this when the definition of functionality doesn't call for negativity? Am I at fault for turning the question into a double-edged sword? I let the functionality question push me to describe what William isn't instead of what he is.

I reread the definition in my head and bring up the positive language that can turn the question's answer into a positive one. William *is* suited to serve a purpose well. In his adult life he serves his purpose at Plowshare every day by stacking the wood, helping others, feeding the animals, taking care of the land, taking the recycling on his bike to the recycling shed, and contributing his spirit and whole self to the community. William has a deep connection with his cousins. He has been my father's sidekick for at least twenty years. He marches with the Temple Town Band. William is set in his ways, and sometimes I wonder if he is the most obnoxious person I know. My answer: William touches your soul with his intuition, his sensitivity, empathy, and honesty.

Humanity

I know a woman who has a son with Trisomy-21. It infuriates her when people confuse our sons for one another. At first, I thought this bothered both of us for the same reason. This woman is outspoken about most things and is a strong advocate for people with special needs. She is fierce, which serves a purpose on one end, but anger and ferocity don't get people far in the long run. Anyway, her son knows the basics of reading and writing, and he speaks French. It pleased me to think we agreed on at least one issue about our sons—just because they have Trisomy-21 doesn't mean they are the same people.

Recently, I learned that our struggle was not mutual. It is not because people don't recognize her son for the unique individual he is. The comparison incenses her because she feels that her son has remarkable cognitive strengths far above William's. She doesn't want people to think her son is like my son based on intelligence and ability.

To her, that matters.

Manifest

Manifest is another verb that creeps up behind me like a dark blanket and smothers everything William is. I don't want to answer how Trisomy-21 manifests because William isn't Trisomy-21. He has it. To manifest is to display, or to show a quality of feeling by one's acts or appearance.

So why don't I relish answering questions about how William displays the characteristics of Trisomy-21? I have been slow to learn that people's curiosity is positive, a yearning to know more as a means of supporting William and me. Still, it puts me on the spot because it needs an answer that describes the syndrome, not my son.

William knows so many people, takes responsibility for his work in his home and community, has a corny sense of humor, and inter-acts with people. I am an introvert, but William is the first to ask me to introduce him to a musician playing at a concert, a police officer, a firefighter, or a passer-by.

I feel pressed to describe the manifestation in general terms. Trisomy-21 manifests itself in the shape of one's eyes, or fine hair, or a thick neck. There may be various anomalies—low muscle tone, a congenital heart defect, a single palmar crease stretching across the middle of his palm—all results of having an extra 21st chromosome. Someone with Trisomy-21, may read and write, or not. He or she may go to college with some adaptation. Some people with Trisomy-21 have heart defects, some live independently, some get married, some have seizures, and early-onset Alzheimer's, some don't.

When someone asks how Trisomy-21 manifests itself, are they asking about William or the syndrome? I want to paint a full picture of who William is. William's approach to the world, which might be unique because he has Trisomy 21, is a combination of who he is, where he is, and what the circumstances are. How Trisomy-21 manifests itself in one person is never going to be the same in another. People with Trisomy-21 may have some similar physical traits, but this has nothing to do with the way they act and feel.

Like with the question of functionality, I need to take the word at face value. When you manifest something, you display qualities and feelings by the way you act. William laughs a lot, likes to trick people, and make them laugh. He skis, listens to music, watches too many movies, rides his bike, and takes rides on the back of his father's motorcycle. William is annoying and kind, serious and silly, loud and quiet. Like many of us, he struggles with change, no matter how big or small. He slows down and examines transitions with scrutiny rather than skimming through them obliviously. His manifestations are infectious.

But You Must!

A friend, who had a daughter with Trisomy-21, once asked me why I wasn't taking William to New York City with my girls and their grandparents. He said, "But you must! You must expose him to everything you can." I can't remember my answer, but I know it wasn't an honest one. His daughter was talented, could read and write, and was a competitor in world gymnastics competitions. She swam and argued articulately with her sisters.

My excuse was that I couldn't take William to New York City because it would be too much work for both of us. Whenever I took William on vacation with the girls, he spent most of the time asking when we were going home. He didn't want to be somewhere unfamiliar. William thrives on routine. Throw in endless subway steps, escalators, and navigating the city, and neither of us will have much fun.

I often caught myself in the threshing machine of wanting William to do what everyone else was excited to do, but not having the patience with his resistance to it. But I need a break. *I* want to keep up with everyone else. *I* want to run over the Brooklyn Bridge or lean over the railing on the New York Harbor cruise. The hermit crabs came back to haunt me. Back then, I could still carry him. But

William became too heavy for me to carry down the subway steps or across the blocks of New York. Besides, he got too old for me to carry him. It was better for both of us to let him stay at home with someone so that he could carry on with his regular routine.

Years later, when William was thirty, I did take him to New York City with his grandfather to see his sister Kate. We took the train down and back. He balked at the escalator, but we found an elevator, and when there were no options, he took the stairs. I made sure to be mindful of pace, and Kate found things he and my father would enjoy. We looked at the city skyline from the banks of the East River. We went to the transit museum. And William had plenty of time to wonder at the whirl of fire trucks, ambulances, and police officers. The highlight of the trip was watching *The Phantom of the Opera* on Broadway. All of us appreciated it, and I am grateful that I grew up enough, so he got the trip he deserved.

The Temple Band

When William and his grandfather go on their forays every Wednesday, the Marine Corps Band pours out of the windows of my father's car announcing their arrival. I don't know whose passion for the Marines Corps Band is greater.

Every summer, the Temple Band, the oldest town band in America, plays marches and medleys at small-town summer concert series in the Monadnock Region. One of my goals for William, years ago, was that he would play in the Temple Band. Each time they played, William insisted on shaking the conductor's hand. It was one of those times that I asked Gordon, the conductor, if William could play with the band.

"Of course," Gordon agreed, "What instrument does he play?"

" 'Corder," William said.

William started rehearsing in the Temple, New Hampshire, town hall in November. After helping the band members set up the chairs, music stands, and percussion, William and I parked ourselves between the timpani and the bass drum. It was there we met Clarisse, who welcomed him as a percussionist. She trusted him with her soft padded drumsticks when the band prepared for the Christmas concert, and if she wasn't there, William played on the big bass drum. I took the back seat, nudging him along if Clarisse was busy with something else. Soon everyone in the percussion ensemble made sure William had something to play—shakers, bells, timpani, snare, and bass drums.

The Christmas concert came and went. Soon it was warm enough for the band to march. William had earned his revolutionary war costume with his authentic tri-corner hat, stockings up to his knees, blue pants, a hand-sewn shirt, and buckled shoes. He stuck with percussion during practice. In parades he plays his recorder. When I told people this, they assumed that William read music and played the recorder proficiently, which is far from the truth. He knew the tunes and had the rhythm, but he didn't know the notes. However, when William turned the recorder to the side to emulate a soldier marching to war, he looked like he was playing along with the band. Although he and I do not have time for rehearsals anymore, he still marches with the Temple Band every summer.

The Whip Lady

"So, this is something real?" I ask.

William repeats the word.

He's telling me that someone is not at band practice. I still don't get it. "Sue, Cecil, Gordon, Connie?"

"NO!" he persists and repeats the name again, flicking his wrist in the air.

"Oh, the whip lady," I sigh. "No, you're right, she's not here." I forget them faster than a person can tell me what their name is, so William and I often make up names. The Whip Lady is the woman who tried snapping a whip in one of our Temple Band Christmas shows to simulate a sleigh driver whipping his team along. I still don't know her name. I dread the day William introduces her.

William and his Grandfather

One problem with my father, and sometimes me, is we tend to have locker room mouths. This is not a good thing, especially with a son as astute as William. He picked up some phrases from me, but more from his grandfather, whose swearing includes the son of God, excrement, and damnation. When William's grandfather says, "Jesus," William finishes with "Christ." Other swear words William has acquired over the years need not be mentioned here. However, this was a genuine concern. I needed to teach him that his grandfather's language was not appropriate. We all need a governor or filter to keep our swearing at bay. My ninety-four-year-old father and my thirty-year-old son are like two adolescents who think swearing is hysterical. When I am with them, I try to keep them in check, but I know they are right back at it when I leave.

Ever since I can remember, my father, Gags, has taken William out to lunch. First, they go to the Peterborough Diner for a greasy cheeseburger, a coke, and chocolate cake—a meal that would horrify their cardiologists. After that, they head for Dunkin' Donuts for a bagel and a Coke. As much as I want to protect William's health, and Dad's, this is their ritual, one that will never change no matter how devious they are about it.

D.C.

When William was eight years old, my father started taking William to the Marine Corps barracks in Washington, D.C., to watch the Marine Corps Band march. He has been taking William there annually ever since. Their tradition developed out of a mutual passion for John Phillips Sousa, parades, and the Marine Corps.

At first, they went alone. Now my father invites the rest of my siblings each year, and one of us goes to make sure the two of them are safe. Always oblivious to traffic, Dad's motto is, "if you walk with confidence, you are invincible." He told me this, years before he lost his hearing, and started to bend over and shuffle across the street, barely making it in the thirty seconds before the light turns red. William tromps alongside. Both of them cross their hands behind their backs, contemplating the bumps in the pavement along the way.

My father always gets to the airport four hours early and leaves William to his own devices. By now, he knows William fears the escalator, so they take the elevator. William and my father, both cardiac risks, spend their idle hours in the airport eating greasy cheeseburgers, a few Dunkin' Donuts, chased by a tall Coke. My father spends the rest of the time reading, and William observes the planes taking off and landing.

My brother John, his son, and I have gone with them for the past three years, but their routine sticks to its regimen. Last year, we got to the barracks three hours early to soothe my father's anxiety about being late. I introduced William to every female Marine I saw because William claims women don't serve. William will argue a point to death, so I decided to get some proof. Marine Corps sergeants, majors, captains, corporals, generals shook his hands. We inspected the cannons and watched the sun start to descend on the crowd.

At the Marine barracks, chiseled young men with cropped hair and women with hair wrapped into tight buns stand erect at the gates, heads covered by crisp white caps with white gloves to match. Uniforms mean a lot to William. The year I joined them on the D.C. trip, he wore the Marine Corps hat and a shirt I bought him for Christmas.

The band marched out in military perfection, led by a female drum major in a giant bearskin hat, not unlike the hats the guards wear at Buckingham Palace. It was magic. One bright star took a prominent space above the steeple, and the Marine Corps carried out their traditional Wednesday night march with absolute precision.

Men and women in sharp straight lines wove in precise formation, and the drill team tossed rifles with bayonets over their shoulders to soldiers on their left, right, and center. It was a three-ring circus, without the chaos. We listened to the silent beat of soldiers catching bayoneted guns in mid-air and tapping them to the ground. Then, the soldiers tossed the guns in unison to the next soldier as they made military formations in the crisp green courtyard of the barracks. The night ended with an overture, including the cannons we had posed by earlier, resonating across the yard. A single beam of light lit up the American flag on the steeple overlooking us as it faded to the sound of taps.

We waited until the rest of the crowd left before navigating our way down the bleachers. The marines lingered loosely. William shook their warm gloves as we passed through the iron gates until next year when we will do it all over again. I wonder if we will. William's grandfather is 94. I cannot fathom William's world without him. There isn't anyone who knows William more and loves him more genuinely than Dad. There isn't anyone who knows my father more and loves him more genuinely than William.

Facing Goliath

As William's graduation from high school grew near, I worried about his future, the great unknown, in a way I was not fearful for my daughters. They knew how to stand up for themselves, and they understood the mysteries of womanhood. They both had chosen a direction—a gap year in Central and South America helping small villages with their schools for Kate, and a year in Chile during high school for Claire. They also had confident voices to make decisions. I knew they could fix a bad choice if they made one. William couldn't.

William turning into a man did not daunt me. I had grown up in a boys' world. I had watched my brothers make this transition along with countless students who graduated from the high school where I taught, and my children learned. What scared me was that I could not always be there for him. I was his translator, his protector, and the one to help him navigate. I had fought like a lioness, but I had also vacillated about the decisions I made for him when he couldn't make them for himself. I had always arranged his world.

Being there for William intertwined family, being a full-time mother, teacher, and living on a shoe-string. If I had had the means, I might have had the money to make different decisions about where he went to school, or who worked with him, or how he developed, but in the long-run, I had traveled a rugged and steep route. William was entering the adult world. I wanted to continue his routine of work and recreation, but this looked different without the school structure. Now my dealings with the Department of Health and Human Services and Medicare would go through me. I was on my own without the community structure that high school had provided for him. I would be finding him a place to live. I would be setting up social situations. It felt as if I was facing a new Goliath as I moved toward finding a future for William that would foster more independence than staying at home.

Turning 21

At the age of 21, everything shifts for people with disabilities. The first thing the state does is determine if they want to have a legal guardian or not. Since William is not capable of making decisions independently, like living alone, handling money, or making medical decisions, Tom and I became his legal guardians.

When one of William's friends, Jeremy, turned 21 two years before William did, the state sent a lawyer to his house. Jeremy opened the door to a lawyer from the state who shot a battery of questions at Jeremy. Did he want a guardian? Perhaps Jeremy would opt out of having a guardian. Then he offered Jeremy some papers to peruse so that he could make his decision. In retelling this event, Jeremy's mother laughed and told me Jeremy responded by asking the lawyer if he had a dog. Jeremy is a smart man. Still, if someone needs guardianship, it is because he or she needs help making big life decisions like this one.

Luckily, Jeremy's parents forewarned me. When William turned 21, I made an appointment with the court instead of having to pay for a lawyer to visit William, as had been the case for Jeremy. The court then appointed a lawyer to represent William on his day in court when a judge would approve or disapprove of our guardianship.

Ironically, a parent has to declare guardianship, but the reasoning is sound. When I asked the lawyer about the purpose of all of this, she told me that sometimes guardians pocket the money meant for a person with a disability for personal use.

In his chambers, the judge asked, "William, do you want your parents to be your guardians?"

"Yes," he replied solemnly. "Mom, he looks like Darth Vader." That was how William determined us as his guardians.

Post-Grad

After William's graduation from high school, my challenge was to integrate him into the community. I had been heading toward this goal for his lifetime. The medical and school institutions had been my training field, now I was on the playing field, gaining on the finish line. It was time to establish him in the adult world.

At 21, CMS funded William's living and medical expenses. I now had two choices. One option was Self-Directed Services, which allowed me to decide where William lived, worked, and carried on with his adult life. The other option was to hand the baton to MDS, who would recommend Monadnock Work Source, which to me, is a daycare for people with disabilities and a dash of *One Flew over the Cuckoo's Nest* mixed into it. I chose Self-Directed Services.

People who choose the government's path usually send their adult children to this local state-funded day program. I sent William there a few times to show the State that William had tried to do it their way. In this program, he spent the day in a self-contained environment where people with disabilities cooked things like packaged pudding, watched movies, played computer games, and sat around. My anxiety increased. I did not want William to be in a self-con-

189

tained program again. I knew that the money the State spent to support this program could be used for something better. My determination reared its head. I was going to make something work.

The challenge of integrating him into the community was an overwhelming responsibility for me. His last five years of school had been smooth sailing. The school found someone to support William, to drive William to work, to help him with his work, and ALLIES was an added bonus. That structure was gone now. I had to create my own, which is not my forte.

Even though Kathy's daughter Emily had one year before she graduated, Kathy and I decided to rent a house for them together in a town west of where I lived at that time. William would live there full-time and Emily would use the house during the day and transition into living there at the end of the school year.

I soon realized that it takes a village to raise a child, but when it comes to adults with disabilities, that is not quite true. The had to build his community using the sources provided by the state and federal government to pay for it. I had to hire someone to live with William. Then I I had to find someone else to support him throughout his day of work and recreation. His day wasn't full, so I had to find other work opportunities for him.

William's transition into adulthood entailed me managing the people who worked with William, working with Kathy to make sure that our shared situation was copasetic, and calling the landlord if anything went wrong with the house. There was also the responsibility of furnishing the house and paying the bills. To find work for William meant convincing an employer to hire him. Finally, I had to find another person to fill in if any of those mentioned above didn't show up.

This was almost a full-time job of coordinating and juggling people to ensure they stayed as long as possible. I still was a full-time teacher, Claire was in middle school, and Tom and I were on the brink of divorce. I was responsible for keeping all of these wheels in motion to make sure William thrived.

He didn't. William's life became a tangle of discombobulated details. He still worked at Edmunds Hardware, the Congregational church, and washed dishes at a nursing home. His social life dwindled to almost nothing. I had to pay people to socialize with him. He didn't know his neighbors and couldn't navigate in his new community independently. William lived next to the fire station in the middle of Peterborough, and the fire whistle beckoning the firefighters to a fire or an accident overwhelmed him so he wouldn't sleep for days afterward.

True Integration

Then I remembered Plowshare. Boyd Quackenbush introduced us to Plowshare when William was born. Boyd was a small, sinewy man—short in stature but grand in presence. He had strong hair and a smile as broad as a barn. He was an anthroposophist, the philosophy upon which Plowshare is based.

Anthroposophy is responsive to the social, human, spiritual, and ecological challenges people face, including those with different abilities. Rudolph Steiner founded Anthroposophy (*anthropo* = human, *sophia* = wisdom). This inspired Dr. Karl Konig, who fled Nazi annexation and moved to Scotland in 1939 with a group of physicians, artists, and caregivers. These people founded the first Camphill community, where they understood and focused on the abilities of each person, not their disabilities. The needs of each person could be met in a cooperative community, with each member contributing his or her own special gifts and talents. (https://www.camphill.org/history/) This vision lives on in a network of one hundred Camphill communities around the world today, of which Plowshare is one.

Boyd lived this philosophy. His property was a maze of organic grains, vegetables, beehives, and apple trees. Everything he owned had a purpose. He planted the trees during the right cycle of the moon or season. Nothing was processed. Everything was natural from apple trees to the fresh milk he got from a local farm. Boyd tended his hives, made apple cider, defended causes, built a shed, or helped someone else build one. Boyd introduced me to Plowshare Farm when William was a baby, and I tucked it in the back of my mind as a possibility for the future.

Finding Home

Boyd took us to a contra dance at Plowshare twenty-nine years ago. Twenty-five years later, Plowshare became William's home. Plowshare Farm is one town away from where I live in Greenfield, New Hampshire. Boyd facilitated its creation so that now people share their lives and nourish the land, which, in turn, feeds the individual tending the land. At Plowshare, care receivers become the caregivers when they work with the animals on the farm, stack the wood, grow and cook the food, fuel the wood furnace, and tend the garden for the community.

Plowshare is an oasis nestled under my favorite mountain, North Pack Monadnock, one of a series in a chain stemming from Mount Monadnock, whose name is derived from an Abenaki word meaning *mountain that stands alone*. Like me, it stands alone but is also a part of a great long chain of people and possibilities that made Plowshare an option for William.

Plowshare fits like a glove. William started going to Plowshare during the day and now lives there full-time. His language and behavior have transformed. There, William has the time to show what work he was cut out for so he could find his niche in the community.

William found his home, and I, for the first time in William's life, didn't worry. As soon as it was possible, he moved into Red House at Plowshare, and he has been there ever since.

At Plowshare, Everyone Dances

When Plowshare has a contra dance, everyone dances. They dance and dance and dance until the rhythm of the caller, the sound of the band, and the laughter become one pulsing, swirling melee of joy. There is a moment when you might wonder how a contra dance could work with such a diverse collection of people.

The music and the dance are tentative and slow until everyone gets used to the moves. Then, those who know the steps, sashay around the room pulling and promenading the rest of us into the dance. The pace picks up, people start to spin, and the magic of the synchronicity sweeps us off our feet.

When the music stops, you can't tell who lives there, who doesn't, who can talk, who can't, who can read, or write, cut wood, smelt ore, weave, paint, or make more music. You know there is magic in the room and don't ever want it to stop.

If I could live on Plowshare Farm, I would. Imagine a place where everyone is expected to do their share, and everyone does. People know what they are capable of contributing, and that's what they do. It takes time to figure out where or how someone can give the most, but that's the beauty of the place. People living at Plowshare Farm make the time to find what fits, and when it does, they join in.

Smelting

At Plowshare, William learned the value of work. When he got there, he tried crafts. My guess is everyone ruled out craftsmanship—he takes after me in that department. William tried gardening for a while, which didn't hold his interest either. He hit the jackpot when he started to work at the cabin with Chris, the blacksmith.

William is not forthcoming when it comes to details about his work life, so I never knew exactly what went on at the cabin. One day my brother and I went to Plowshare to find out. We found Chris blacksmithing on his own. He explained the process of smelting and the role William played in the process.

A group of workers walks to the base of North Pack Monadnock to the cabin where they melt the magnetite mined by Chris. Using a Japanese smelting technique (handcraftvillage.com/metal-work), they reduce the iron from its ore and forge the resulting metal into musical instruments. To do that, they need to keep a fire going. William manages the wood. He finds saplings from one to two inches in diameter, cuts them down, saws them into foot-long sticks, and stacks them. Then they make charcoal out of the wood to smelt the ore. Once the ore oozes out of the kiln Chris built, they mold it into flute-like instruments to sell at Local Share in Wilton.

The complexity of this process and the tangible final result of the work that goes into it is remarkable. What is more impressive is the role everyone plays. It works like the contra dance, first with tentative steps. Gradually, those who know the steps pull William into the dance of work. At the cabin, he experiences the value of work that goes way beyond payment or a tangible reward.

High Scrutiny

In the late eighties, when William was born, the federal government, fortunately, mandated the closure of all state mental institutions. New Hampshire was ahead of its time in freeing people with disabilities from its state institution and supporting group homes instead. The state established area agencies and gave individuals with developmental disabilities and acquired brain disorders support and services in the community. This gave birth to the group home, which houses four to sixteen people with disabilities. People have daily jobs or activities outside of the home with a one to one aide. Group homes are closer to the public school model where people's abilities are *not* the purpose of their existence. The majority of group homes meet the criteria that CMS supports.

Plowshare is the most inclusive setting William has been in since pre-school. At Plowshare, families live together with their spouses, children, and other community members. People are free to come and go as they please after a day of work on the farm. No one follows them around, waiting for them to make a mistake. At Plowshare, people work side by side with the land to grow the food they eat or chop the wood that warms them.

In 2014 the federal government gave individual states the deadline of 2020 to develop their rules on integration and bring them into alignment with the federal government. For several states, that means closing institutions as New Hampshire did in the eighties. Because of the federal mandate, the state put Plowshare under high scrutiny because the regulations frown upon farm communities, which had the potential to foster forced labor. Also, since many people with disabilities live at Plowshare Farm, they do not line up with the guidelines for integration in the community.

What should matter is what people do at Plowshare and how it integrates people from all walks of life. Yet, if these regulations threaten to tear apart the fabric of Plowshare's being, Plowshare could choose to refuse state funding. Most people can pay for Plowshare out-of-pocket. However, William and six others rely on CMS funding to pay their room and board and other expenses.

If the state decides that Plowshare does not meet its criteria for integration, CMS would not fund William to live there. If this happens, William would be right back where we started when we tried inclusive living in downtown Peterborough. Everything I have spent his life fighting for so that William could live the rich and full life he lives could evaporate.

The Conundrum Rears
its Head Again

I would love it if it took a village to raise William, and it has to an extent. It does take a village to support the people who don't have a voice in their destiny. But the world isn't ready to do this yet. Full inclusion cannot happen in a day. Our communities and our economy are not prepared to support people with different abilities.

Things are moving, but slowly. CMS states, "family members have been encouraging the federal government to support people living within their communities for thirty-five years." However, this full-inclusion model does not work for me because I want William to have authentic and not contrived connections with people. People choose to live in a life-sharing community because they want to share their lives, contributing to a close-knit cooperative community.

William needs guidance when he works. At Plowshare, no one is paid to make William work. Everyone works side by side and supports each other. One of William's jobs is to load the truck with firewood. Everyone in the group needs his help to get the job done. His reward for working at Plowshare is camaraderie and staying warm in the winter.

If he were working in town, he would have to work at a place that was willing to hire him, not at a job that he likes or chooses to do. Then, the aide who is paid to work with him would try to get him to do the work. His reward, if he is lucky, is a paycheck, which is rare. Because society hasn't erased the stigma that follows people with disabilities, the system prefers to support a one-size-fits-all approach. The system that CMS approves places people in situations without having any idea what his or her preference is. Plowshare puts the individual first. The system puts the system first.

One person who was raised in a life-sharing community and lives in William's house at Plowshare says, "living here supports humanity. We *are* humanity, and we need to live humanely—supporting each other in our work, our living, and our society. Plowshare is a model of how the world should live."

Currently, until CMS comes to their decision, people like William can use their funding for the same privilege as those who could afford to pay for it out of pocket. This funding supports a lifestyle that gives him dignity and self-worth.

My Plea

In a letter to the Department of Health and Human Services, I asked what will happen if Plowshare will not comply with their regulations? How will William feel if he couldn't live there because someone thought his home didn't fit the criteria set by a government official? Where else could he go where he could support the people he loves?

CMS replied that the rule does not prohibit people from living in places like Plowshare. However, "a setting like Plowshare needs to be reviewed with high scrutiny to ensure that CMS funded services support an individual's ability to access and participate in the broader community."

In the letter I wrote, I also added, "William doesn't have a voice to defend himself or to ask government officials to continue funding him to stay in a place that took twenty-five years for him to find. I am his voice. I ask you to understand the value of Plowshare Farm for the community it is, for the outside community it serves. William and his peers deserve to choose where they live like any other citizen in this country."

Wonder Woman

I am an actress
exuding strength from the master stage.
The teacher
who stopped being strong and started being herself.
The mother
who ran away when she thought she could.
That woman—
That Amazon
realized being an Amazon is
a
show—
a charade.

That woman lies swaddled on the living room floor
Small and trapped
too afraid to move
in the deep dark of the night
the fear so overwhelming she can't
stop.

No breath
Frozen
Until
like the Iceman Cometh,
she
breaks
out.

She wishes she were a bird—
not a plane carrying people inside of her
A simple yellow bird flitting across the river
Lifted with the rest of the flock.

My Walkabout

William settled at Plowshare in 2014, and it seemed the high scrutiny issue had simmered down, which gave me time to think about where my own life was headed. I had been divorced for six years and involved in another relationship for two of those years. My passion for classroom teaching was waning. Teaching was spilling into my life and leaving a bitter taste behind. It felt like I was on a hamster's wheel. So, I jumped. I gathered my courage and resigned from where I was teaching. I had the choice to teach there for another ten years and collect a decent pension or to take a risk and try something new. My three children were settled in their careers and resided where they chose to live; now it was my turn.

I chose to head to Tampico, Mexico, to continue teaching for one-half of the salary I earned in the United States. I went there to teach, but also to seek adventure. This was the first time I had left my family, but it was also the first time they had left me. Kate had graduated from college, Claire was studying to be a nurse, and William was at Plowshare.

Someone asked a friend of mine when I left for Mexico, "How could she have left William?" Hearing that sent a jolt of guilt through me. My friend told them I needed this walkabout, but I am not sure she knew how to respond to my exodus either. I left Kate and Claire too. I wasn't under trial for that. But how could I have left William? I felt relieved of my duty to fight for him because I had reached the lifelong goal of finding a place where he belonged. Was it so awful I left William, my roots, my job, my family, and everything I owned for three years? I saw a chance to leap into adventure, and I took it.

Besides, I wasn't thinking about leaving William. It was an impulse. I needed to get away. Something crawled inside of my head and said it is time to think about yourself, take a walkabout, see the world, find out who you are while you can.

My walkabout took me far. After a year in Mexico, an e-learning company in Kuala Lumpur, Malaysia, hired me as a Subject Matter Expert, which meant writing online lessons for ESL students. I sold my house in New Hampshire and gave away all of my possessions. I needed to shed my responsibilities and focus on myself.

Time to return

I had been working in Malaysia for two years when I received an email from Plowshare describing an episode William had with a seizure-like headache. Plowshare had called Tom after William had collapsed in the barn. Coincidentally, I called Tom when he was in the ER with William. "Have you told the ER doctor about William's heart condition, Tom." I yearned to be on the other side of the line and the world right then.

He put on the doctor who said, "Oh, that explains it. We will put a temporary heart monitor on him and send the results to Dr. Flanagan." The ER doctor stuck a disposable heart monitor on William's chest with an adhesive as strong as worn out Scotch tape.

At Plowshare, William ripped off the monitor as soon as he could. Kay, who ran William's house, managed his prescriptions, and was his dear friend, among other things, would replace it, and he would pull it off. On. Off. On. Off. One night, I Skyped William as I did every week. It took an hour for me to cajole him into putting on the monitor again. As soon as I hung up, off it came. I told Kay to give up. This was not going to work. By the looks of William, the object on his chest with a blinking green light terrified him.

I wasn't there for him when he had these episodes. But the Plowshare community was. The what-ifs scared me. What if someone wasn't there for him? What if this happened in his sleep? My anxiety went wild with building what-ifs. This was enough for me to start considering my return home.

One night I awoke in Malaysia knowing I needed to go home. It did not feel like this was the end of my walkabout. Perhaps it was the beginning of a new one or the continuation of the circle. I had to come back for my family, my three children, and my peace of mind. As I approached my sixth decade, and William approached his third, I returned from my three-year walkabout to Mexico, then Malaysia, and back.

Getting to the Heart
of the Matter

Why was William keeling over when he sat on a bench? Why was he crumbling in a heap at random moments? Why were these episodes becoming more frequent? For years, William had what I thought were headaches. He didn't express them as such. I assumed when he held his head, and it looked like a sharp pain was going through it, he was experiencing a headache. When William was in middle school, Tom and I had taken him to a headache specialist. He shrugged and told us there is not much we can do about chronic headaches. I don't know why I didn't pursue it further. I come from a headache family where headaches come and go. Why should William be any different? This time I had a strong feeling something was wrong with his heart. Ever since his first heart surgery, I knew the probability of something going wrong with his heart would come back to bite us.

The Return

In the twenty-four hours that it took to fly from Kuala Lumpur, Malaysia, to Boston, Massachusetts, I fell into a deep depressive state. I had stopped taking my medication in Malaysia, thinking I could meditate my darkness away and that I was strong enough to beat it myself. But now it was out of control and all-consuming. I had to face my demon as I had tried to many times before. This time I couldn't win.

Three days after I had landed in the States, my father, brother, William, and I took our annual trip to see the Marine Corps band in August. I had called his cardiologist before we left, and the nurse returned the call while I was standing on the Washington Mall in the stifling afternoon heat.

"I want to set up an appointment with Dr. Flanagan as soon as possible," I told the nurse on the other end of the line. "William has been fainting and passing out, and I think there is something wrong with his heart."

"But he is not due for his cardiac check-up until next year."

It was hard to believe that I had any tears left, but they poured out. "Can't we push the appointment to one year earlier?" I gulped, too worn out to fight. To my relief, the nurse agreed and squeezed William in for an October appointment. It was reaching the end of August. I managed to find a place to stay in a house that belonged to a friend of my mother. This friend's husband recently died, and she welcomed the company. I was working remotely for Learning Port in Malaysia, but I knew that would not last, and the reverse culture shock took me by surprise.

Leaning in

October rolled around. I took William to Dr. Flanagan, the cardiologist who had fixed William's heart when he was a month and a half old. He had moved up north from Children's Hospital in Boston.

"William," he asked, "Do you ever feel dizzy?"

I leaned in, "He does when he falls off benches and passes out." William doesn't like to admit that he feels ill. It's as if he thinks he has done something wrong if he doesn't feel well.

"Well," Dr. Flanagan said, "The reading on his heart monitor shows no signs of unusual activity." He was referring to the monitor that the ER doctor had given William while I was in Malaysia. The monitor that William refused to wear.

"What?" I almost screamed. "There is no reading on the heart monitor because William never had the monitor on for more than a minute before he ripped it off. I sent it back to the lab because we gave up on it."

"The results say that he had it on for three days, long enough for us to get a reading on his heart activity," Dr. Flanagan replied in his always soft, pensive voice.

"Could you please bring up the reading and show it to me?" There was no way they had a reading. I knew this.

"Hmmm." Dr. Flanagan raised his bushy eyebrows. "You are right. There is no reading. Maybe we should try the heart monitor again."

This was an OMG moment. A moment when I could have jumped on his desk and screamed, ARE YOU SERIOUS? But I had come to learn that this was common in medical, educational, and social services. My brief interlude from bureaucracy had made me forget that for a moment. I trusted Dr. Flanagan with William's life and my soul. Even he could over-look something as serious as a misread.

"Okay," I resigned, knowing the effort was a lost cause, but having the faintest glimmer of optimism. "The only way we can make William keep the monitor on is if you have tape stronger than Duct tape to secure it."

"Our nurse can do that," he assured me. "I also think you should schedule an appointment with Neurology to rule out epilepsy."

I trust Dr. Flanagan. If he said William needed to wear a heart mon-itor, he needed it to wear it. "Okay, we can give it another try."

Dr. Flanagan left, and in came the heart monitor nurse. She was all about heart monitors. However, I didn't see any hard-core tape in her hands and said so.

"We don't have any tape like that," she responded.

I thought, and it shows a lot of development on my part that I didn't blow a gasket, *this is the biggest hospital in New Hampshire, and you don't have any tape stronger than that?* Instead, I questioned, "You don't have anything more than the sticky stuff on the back of the heart monitor?" Already my mind was racing ahead. I learned long ago when a professional tells me she can't do something requiring common sense, I have to figure it out myself.

"We can put this over it," she suggested pulling a wide floppy ban-dage out of a drawer.

"Sure," I said, assuming the pharmacy downstairs would have Kinesio tape that athletes use for healing and supporting injuries.

It didn't.

We made it to the car. William furrowed his brow in his fury at having to wear the heart monitor, but he hadn't ripped it off—yet. I coached him about how important it was for him to keep the monitor on—how it was going to make him better, how it was going to make him stop fainting. I pulled into a sports store ten minutes later. "Do you have any Kinesio tape?"

"Yes."

I bought it and asked where the fitting room was. I told William to take off his shirt. Then I strapped on that heart monitor with an entire roll of Kinesio tape. I was going to win this time. How many times have I thought I could win at things William had his mind set on not doing? I must have been in an altered state.

William brooded the whole way home, but he kept the monitor on under miles of tape.

I dropped him off at his house.

That night I got a call. He had ripped the monitor off in the shower.

Facing the Demon

During the six months while I was trying to find the answers to William's fainting problem, I cried incessantly and wondered if I could go on with my life. I had come back home to help William, who would have died if I hadn't returned. I didn't realize I would have to take care of myself as well. Still, I set up appointments for cardiology and neurology at the great hospital of the North. And waited. And cried.

By March, I was unraveled. I spent four days in the hospital, which helped to get me back on a minuscule dose of antidepressant and anxiety medication. I had to wait three months to see a psychiatrist who would adjust the prescription, so it would actually work, and another six weeks until the drugs took effect. The medical system works in the psychological world as it does in William's world of medicine and government mandates.

Depression of this caliber is the toughest life-long hurdle I have to confront whenever it chooses to rear its ugly head. And like Trisomy-21, depression doesn't go away. I will never be cured of this illness. I will relapse, as I have before. However, it is manageable with a lot of therapy, understanding from friends and family, and medicine.

One-way understanding

Will you be my legacy, or will I be yours? What is going on in your heart that doctors can't figure out? Does anyone else worry the way I do? Do they want to believe the neurologist's speculation about epilepsy?

We had hardly sat down and introduced ourselves before the neurologist said, "William has epilepsy because he has Down syndrome." as if that is enough of a reason, and then he backed up his edict and continued: "he will have Alzheimer's within a few decades." Did he know you were there? Did he hear me reassure you that everything would be okay? Did this doctor see the fear in your expression? What did you hear? What did you understand?

"What if I don't want to believe you?" I challenged one of the most renowned neurologists in the state. "How can you convince me you are right?" I almost stamped my feet to show him my defiance. The neurologist shrugged his box-like shoulders, considered us with darkened eyelids, and told us he knew these things. You looked as scared as I felt.

I still think it's your heart. Ever since those big doctors fixed you when you were small, I have anticipated the day something would go wrong. It was too easy to walk out of Children's Hospital twenty-nine years ago without glancing back.

Now, you and I have to look forward. The neurologist says it's epilepsy because it's easier for him to assume that epilepsy comes hand in hand with Trisomy-21. What if it isn't, and we are waiting too long to figure out if it *is* your heart? I wish you would let them monitor your heart the easy way. Just strap on the monitor and not be afraid, if that is what you are. Why don't you want to find the truth about what is happening to you? How can I make you understand this could be a lifesaver? A heart monitor could give us an answer and then a solution. How can I know if you understand?

One of the directors at Plowshare, in her anthroposophical way, suggested that maybe I need to let you live your life in your body with all of its foibles. When you are ready, you can find your heaven where you can be happy and at peace without having to go through what it would take to fix you. I don't want to see it that way. As if your leaving me could ever be a good thing.

I will be patient, even though patience scares me, especially now. I will let the neurologist with box-like shoulders prescribe Keppra, an EEG, and an MRI. We will wait and see if you have another seizure. I hope you don't because that will be our evidence that it is your heart. If the medicine works, then you have epilepsy. But if it doesn't, if you do have another episode, then everything points to your heart. That means we will need to sew a heart monitor into your chest.

Do you understand?

From Plumbing
to Electricity

William fainted one week after we met with the neurologist, who was still determined he was right about his diagnosis despite his continuing fainting episodes. Finally, six months after I returned from Malaysia in August, Dr. Flanagan was in favor of implanting a heart monitor. He did have to pass William on to another doctor. "You see," he explained. "I am the plumber. I take care of the way the blood pumps through the heart. William needs an electrician to fix his heart this time."

Why was there a raging snowstorm whenever I drove William the hour and a half north to the hospital? The tension of driving through blinding snow and not making it to the appointment on time mounted higher than the snow collecting on the highway, but we made it.

William lit up the cardiac unit, like the sun spreading across the living room floor in the afternoon. Each patient, worn out by life and a heart that turned them grey, turned a shade brighter as William strode by them. He was the only strong and youthful one in the unit.

It reminded me of the many parades in which he had marched with the same confidence.

The medical staff whirled in and out of his room. This team was made up of doctors, nurses, and interns responsible for every aspect of his heart—his respiration, his consciousness, his incision, and the pacemaker. As usual, it was as if they were speaking in tongues. But I got the gist. They were going to put William under general anesthesia, insert a heart monitor under his skin and above the heart, maneuver a wire through his blood vessels to attach to his heart, and close him up again. Then we would wait to see how the monitor would read William's next episode.

Translation

I am William's translator, especially when William is in the hospital, where doctors and nurses focus on his heart and how to fix him instead of what he embodies. The last specialist to come in before inserting the heart monitor was the anesthesiologist.

"I'm Will," William said, offering his hand for the anesthesiologist to shake as he started to poke and prod William's abdomen. The anesthesiologist continued his work. When William continued to hold out his hand, he stopped prodding and looked at me.

"He said, 'I'm Will,'" I translated.

William followed with, "Who are you?"

"He wants to know who you are." Despite the levity in his voice, William's expression was serious. "Mom, that guy has a beard," William told me.

"Yup," I replied, "he does." The intern with the scraggly beard looked up at me as he pressed William's belly, beyond tickling.

"He says you have a beard."

"He should shave."

I translated this to the anesthesiologist who looked up and scratched his beard with his free hand.

"Yea, I suppose I should."

"You can use my razor." The anesthesiologist's eyes widened. He took his hands off William and laughed.

Something I Hadn't Considered

Before William came out of recovery, the heart monitor special-ist approached me with a box and showed me into a side room. I was still in the throes of depression, so I warned her, "I want you to know I will cry but do not take it personally. It is what I do." When I saw the box, I realized that there was more to inserting the heart monitor than I thought. I had been so caught up in the surgery itself. I hadn't thought about the monitor that would record the beats of William's heart and transfer the information to some dark room where people stared at screens of hearts all day.

The specialist gave me an awkward look and pulled out the contents of the box. What she pulled out looked like a router but sleeker. I had shut down before she opened her mouth. She plunged into her spiel about how William would have to take a device that looked like a wand with a circle at the end of it, wave it over his heart once, then wave it over...

"That's not going to happen," I interrupted her through my tears. I may have been depressed, but I wasn't stupid. She had met

William, talked to William, and thought William could do all of this? "You are going to have to set up the monitor here because he won't let me do it, and he cannot do it on his own," I said with tears pouring down in sheets. Yet another set of blinking lights was not going to bode well with William.

"Oh no, I can't do that," the specialist stammered. I had interrupted her rote recitation of the instructions and left her flustered and undone. She was like a telemarketer who knew what she had to say, but to take responsibility for her words was far beyond her reach.

"Why not? I stuttered through voiceless tears.

"We don't have cell service here."

I didn't say it, but that was a downright lie. I had four bars on my phone and had spent enough time in that hospital to know they had cell service.

"Well, you are going to have to figure out that one," I told her. And she did. I had given over my problem-solving skills and handed them to her.

Back at the Farm

After his surgery, I knew William might rip off his bandage, but knew he would not be able to pull the heart monitor out of his chest. Upon my return to William's house, his housemates distracted him while I set up the monitor. It would load William's heart activity every twenty-four hours and report it wirelessly to the hospital seventy miles north.

His housemates drifted into William's room to find me moving William's bureau two inches to the right so I could plug in the monitor. I covered it with a cloth and hid it surreptitiously underneath the bureau before William saw it. We shook our heads. This was not going to work. They laughed. I was too tired to cry.

William places everything he owns in his room with precision. For twenty-four years of his life, his books, bed, bureau, and CD player never moved. They left dents in the carpet so that when I vacuumed his room, I would be able to place things where they had stood before. If someone moved anything by a hair, he was sure to let everyone know about it. One of his housemates earned the epithet, "she who went into my room." He hits one index finger with the other to enunciate the point.

When William walked into his room, he noticed I had moved the bureau and hidden the monitor under it. "William, you cannot move this monitor." I was under strict instructions from the heart monitor woman to position it eight feet from William's bed—another piece of misinformation I would learn about later.

Two days later, I went back to William's room to see if everything was in order. William was working on the farm, so I slipped into his room and looked under his bureau. The monitor was gone. The box it came in, which I had hidden far underneath his bed, was gone too. I scoured his room, then the house trash. A housemate came in and said, "William, always takes things that don't belong to the recycling bin in the barn." We looked in the house recycling, then in the recycled trash for all of Plowshare, and found the empty box, but no monitor. I left. This was beyond my capacity.

That night I got a call from Plowshare. William had fessed up to hiding the monitor in the back of a closet in the kitchen. The monitor had been unplugged and moved around so much at this point I was sure it couldn't be working. A month later, I found out I was wrong.

Reprieve

William jingled the bells in the Temple Band Christmas concert, while the snow fluttered down and coated the roads with a perilous layer of slush and ice. Before the weather went wrong, his grandfather and I had promised to take him out for dinner. I couldn't bear to change the schedule for him, but the two places we wanted to go were closed, so I had to drive him home. He growled disappointment and resisted getting in the car. These moments of resistance make me want to force him into the car, to hurry him along because I am cold and tired. I think, and sometimes say, *please don't do this to me, William, just get in the car*. I suppose that is how Trisomy-21 manifests itself in me.

When we got to Red House, where he lives on Plowshare Farm, no one was home, which threw William further into the unknown. It was cold and icy, and I wasn't sure what to do until a woman showed up and told me everyone was eating dinner at Jovis, the house next to William's. The standard trajectory of a Sunday evening at Plowshare Farm had taken yet another direction.

William sat as stiff as a statue in my car and put on his I-am-not-going-to-budge stance. I took a deep breath and exhaled slowly.

Inhaling pulled me into his mindset. He wanted to stay with his grandfather, with me, to eat at the restaurant. Then, he had to shift gears to go home and have dinner at his house. The snowfall increased while his brain caught up to the next transition of eating in yet another place.

I told him I knew how hard it was for him, guided him to Jovis, and drove away. I cannot make life easy for William because life *is* hard. It is full of transitions most of us glide through without noticing.

New Year

The weather was kind when I took William for his follow-up visit with the neurologist. I don't know why we were going back. We had proof of another fainting episode and knew he did not have epilepsy. I was prepared to wean him off the Keppra the minute I stepped into the neurologist's office when he arrived two hours late.

When the neurologist settled into his chair and pulled up William's chart on the screen, he went into a frenzy. "What is this? This can't be right," he ranted as William and I, terrified, watched him clicking the keyboard as if to make the screen say something else.

I managed to sputter, "What's wrong?"

"But this can't be true." The neurologist stammered. "It's inaccurate. He was having seizures. This is a misreading."

William's eyes darted from one of us to the next.

"What?" I said, standing up to read the screen.

"It says here that William's heart stopped beating for 30 seconds on December twenty-fourth at 5:30 am." It was now January fifth.

After a series of frantic calls, we paged Dr. Flanagan, who once again came to our rescue. He said he needed to research the issue and would get back to me the next day. True to his word, Dr. Flanagan called at three the following afternoon. After about ten minutes of medical speak, I said, "So if William's heart *did* stop beating for 30 seconds on December twenty-fourth while he was sleeping, what does this mean?"

"It means," Dr. Flanagan's steady voice said, "you need to come up here right away. If his heart stops beating again, it may not start up again as it has before."

I mulled it over for a minute. I was tired from crying all day. William would be rattled by this. I didn't want to rush and create panic for either one of us. It was my turn to pause. I paused because I knew that the tension of driving to the hospital right away was not worth the stress it would put on William and me. Besides, I knew well enough it would be best to stay at home while the hospital found William a bed before we trudged up there and sat in the waiting room until they did. This time the call for action was to be calm. William had been having these episodes for one year, maybe more in his sleep, and another night wouldn't hurt. We both needed to gear up for this one.

"I'll be there in the morning."

Dear William,

On the EKG, your heart was a series of squiggles that weren't squiggling the way they should. Instead, they lay flat for 30 long seconds in the middle of the night, or while you fell to the ground as you loaded the truck with wood, or accordioned to the barn floor while you tended the cows. But something inside of you woke up your heart each time. Something inside you said, "I am not stopping here."

Yesterday, they fixed the electricity in your heart. You were mad about the giant bandage that had to sit on your chest all week. The wires would be there forever. You could feel the pacemaker underneath your skin living inside of you and sending your heart's electrical signals north every day.

After they inserted your pacemaker, your chest was swollen. There was something unreal inside of you. When you got home, you didn't eat your plateful of food. Your eyes were like dark hollow tunnels traveling to the root of the pain. Your furrowed brow knitted the anxiety swirling inside of you. Your husky voice yelled, "It hurts! No! Don't! Don't touch. It hurts." I held you as I held you when you were a child. We rocked. "I know it hurts. I am sorry it hurts. Things hurt sometimes." Solving problems hurts.

That night as I started to leave, someone asked you to thank me for all I do for you. "Tell her how much you love her," she coaxed.

Express the nonverbal with words.

"Mom." You called me back.

"Mom," you said, and you waited.

I waited and leaned into you.

We touched foreheads.

You didn't need to say a word.

Reconnecting

I expected a routine check-up. The kind when you drive an hour and a half so a technician can tell you the pacemaker was working. It wasn't. The wire in the lower ventricle had not adhered to tissue and settled the way it should have. It takes six weeks for the wires to adhere to the heart. As long as you don't lift your hands over your shoulders or do any heavy lifting. William sleeps with his hands under his head. He puts his coat on by laying it on the floor, putting his hands into the sleeves, and whipping it over his head. Perhaps, I hadn't emphasized how essential it was that William not do this.

William would have to go through another surgery to reconnect the wire from his pacemaker to his heart again. It was more straightforward this time because they only had to reattach one wire, and the pacemaker was already in place. The surgeon didn't have to trace William's complicated mass of blood vessels to his heart again; he reattached the dangling wires. This time William got to go right home, and the device that read his heart was tucked and secure under his bureau. There would be no repeat performance of the disappearing heart monitor.

Weeks later, the hospital called me to ask if William was undergoing intense exercise because the reading on his monitor was sending messages that his heart was racing. He wasn't. Even if he had been, it wouldn't have pushed his resting pulse to 170. William had called me the night before complaining of a stomach ache, which wasn't typical for him, so I had an inkling something was wrong. After William got into my car to make another trip to the hospital, I asked him where his stomach ache hurt. He pointed to his chest. He didn't look well.

We drove to the tunes of *The Music Man* and *Raffi* as a sense of fear settled into the car. It is never a good thing when the hospital tells you to get there on the double. This time a pause was not an option. I could see his heart fluttering against his T-shirt. We arrived at 5:00 on a Friday afternoon after most of the doctors left, and the staff was at a minimum. Friday is the worst time to get to the hospital when you need immediate care, which William did.

There was too much silence as the doctor tried to override William's tachycardia with his pacemaker. If the pacemaker could force his lower ventricle to catch up to his upper ventricle's 360 pulses per minute, it could override it. Then the rhythm of William's heart could readjust. When that didn't happen, it was the doctor's turn to readjust. It didn't take long to admit William to the ER and recharge his heart. In the old days, they would have used paddles and said "clear" the way they do on *Grey's Anatomy*. Now they use oversized rectangular patches—one patch sticks on the front and another one on the back. That was all I knew because I couldn't stay for the five minutes it took to stop and restart his heart.

One of the doctors, who seemed to be in charge of the recharge, told us we would go home that night. Others weren't so sure. William was adamant. "I am not spending the night." We spent hours in that state. "I'm not staying here. I'm not sleeping here. I'm going home." On the page, his words sound gentle, but they were dark and hollow.

I wasn't sure what to say to William until one doctor on his team confirmed we were leaving. The nurse unplugged the wires attaching William to the EKG, his pulse, his oxygen, and heart monitor. I was relieved I didn't have to explain anything to William, and we could put an end to the visit and head home. However, my relief was premature.

An hour later, a different doctor came in to tell us William wasn't going anywhere—for the next four days. It is not uncommon for one person on a medical team to say one thing and another person to say something else. William was furious, and I felt the gravity of the situation leak onto the floor. He needed close monitoring to make sure the new medicine worked and that his heart would keep beating at a reasonable pace.

When we left four days later, it didn't feel as if I had put an end to the medical troubles William will have to face as an adult. Life is catching up to William and me. For now, he is well; his heart beats steadily under his shirt. He has a new bike, a new scar, and more medicine to add to his repertoire for hypothyroidism and high blood pressure. I discovered that we did not have to store the monitor under his bed. I had been misinformed. He needs to be close to it 20 minutes a day, so it sits in the dining room without drawing notice, so that it can send William's heartbeats north every day.

Do They All
Look the Same?

I would love to think William's story is not necessary. Almost every day someone reminds me with a stare, a question, or comment, that perspectives on Trisomy-21 haven't changed much since William was born. I am not sure why. People with Trisomy-21 were liberated from institutions almost 30 years ago. They live longer, go to school, reside at home, and later in vibrant communities. Many people still lack the awareness of how different people with Trisomy-21 are from each other. Their capabilities vary, and, like all of us, their intellect is as broad as the typical population. It seems people sometimes forget that they are human.

Friends and members of the community continue to mistake William for another man with Trisomy-21 who lives in our town. This man is five years younger than William. He dresses well, and he never looks like he has been working on a farm, as William does. This man has chosen to live independently, and he plays a drum and chants to its beat in various places around town.

It's not okay for people to mistake two people because they have similar traits. I can think of many racist remarks starting with "I can't tell those (fill in the race) apart. They all look the same to me." It's the same thing with Trisomy-21.

One day, William was playing with the Temple Band as the rain thrummed on an unsteady green and white striped tent. A woman, neither of us knew, started calling "JOSIAH, JOSIAH." William didn't turn around because he isn't Josiah. Besides, he was performing. William looked like Josiah because Josiah has Trisomy-21. Maybe if I weren't still in the throes of depression or recovering from a year of almost losing my son, I would have made this a teachable moment. But even that was a stretch. So, instead, I lost it. "He is not Josiah. He doesn't know Josiah."

"Oh, but he looks just like Josiah," she beamed as if I must be mistaken. "Josiah just graduated from high school, and everyone loves him so much," she gushed.

"His name is William, and he is turning 30," I snarled. "You know *they* are not all the same because *they* have Trisomy-21." I turned my back to close the conversation and stewed, not at the woman, but at myself. I was ashamed of myself for reacting to an innocent woman. She didn't know how many times this happened to William. She didn't know this was a sore subject for people who have the traits of Trisomy-21, but still have different hair, different smiles, different clothes, and everything else that makes someone unique. Finally, I got up and sidled through the soggy crowd to find the woman. I got to her eye level and said, "I am sorry. I was way out of line speaking to you in that tone. It is common for people to mistake William for other people with Trisomy-21, and this time it got to me."

"Oh, that's okay," she chortled. "He is just like Josiah though…"

"I am really sorry," I said and walked away.

Do you Know?

William,
Do you know
that you touch people like the morning dew?
I know what I know.

You bring light
as if you were skimming by the opposing
team at the end of a soccer game
slapping hands sideways with each opposing player.

as if you were a time-lapse of city lights spreading across the world
until the whole earth filled with the light of you

as if you were the force of the sun making a shadow
of the tip of a mountain disappear at sunrise
when everyone reaches the top but you.

Did you let yourself happen—
opening up like a human flower
not as graceful
when you refused to grow like one.

Someone once told me God sent you to me.
She didn't mean God.
She meant something that sends angels to troubled souls
To teach them what you taught me.

Puttering

William pulls back my throttle until I settle into his pace. He steers me away toward vigilant, compassionate, and mindful waters where we putter along with the current. His world is timeless. Today, he measures time by what day he stacks the wood, when he works in the barn, what night is music night, or what day one of his co-workers has off. William's way of moving through life is to taste it, chew it, ponder it, and absorb it before he digests it.

Renewal

Experts say William will die before I do. It's a reality they try to make me believe. So anytime you consider asking, "don't people like William have short lifespans?" Remember that my heart sinks. I want to ask, "Are you human?"

Your heart is tangled with its many repairs Still, it holds all that you share with the world. And I am a simple tangled mom.

Yesterday, I walked through the woods and up to Mt. Skatutakee on the same path I used to carry William up on my back. My naked Vibram soles slid up the mountainside. My micro-spikes dangled and clattered outside of my pack, reminding me that if I put them on, it would make the trip easier. I refused their clanking suggestions. I wanted to slip and slide—defying the gravity of challenges.

Every time I looked up, the woods, the woods, echoed in my head. "What happened to you?" I asked them on this post-winter day. "You are grey, gloomy, and cold." Deadwood and rotten debris crisscrossed in jumbled dark and gray piles on the snow. The winter's destruction was natural, blameless, part of the life cycle. Tiny handprints of lost possums gave me the hope that something so small could make something so safe and sure. I kept my eyes riveted to their delicate handprints. I thought, are they looking at me looking for them? Are the squirrels chattering at me because what I see are not possum prints at all?

Everything dies. There is always renewal in the spring. William may not be renewed someday. His life has been a complicated crisscross of joy, confusion, and systems set up like tiny boxing rings. Sometimes a clatter of negative challenges added to an already heavy burden, and the pain of sliding down a slippery slope taught me how to manage what is most valuable in life's cycle.

I am always ahead of William's tracks, treading a path to make it easier for him to follow. No one knows the joy hidden underneath the path. The millions of times those who cleared the way trod it, along with those who may have been reluctant. I am a mountain climber, a woman of the woods. It is what I do. None of William's life has been a sacrifice for me. William is the part of the climb I hope will never end as long as I am on this earth.

Works Cited

Kingsley, Emily Perl. "Welcome to Holland." www.pdx.edu/students-with-children/sites/www.pdx.edu.students-with-children/files/Welcome%20to%20Holland.pdf

Pradhan, Mandakini et al. "Fertility in men with Down syndrome: a case report." *Fertility and sterility* vol. 86,6 (2006): 1765.e1-3. doi:10.1016/j.fertnstert.2006.03.071

"Understanding Inclusion."*Special Education Guide.* www.specialeducationguide.com/pre-k-12/inclusion/whats-inclusion-theory-and-practice/

Acknowledgments

Don Metz
Denise Cloutier
Deni Dickler
Don Metz
Margaret Carlson
Beth Corwin
Susan Knight
Thomas P
Aunt Phoebe
Kate Gleason
Tuesday Writing Group in Keene
Keene Writers in Library
Elm City Writers
Monadnock Writers' Group
Carl Mabb-Zeno
Greenfield writing group
Peggy Brown
LouAnne Beauregard

Made in United States
North Haven, CT
12 October 2021

10285000R00150